Trip to Tanzania

Julie Jane

authorHOUSE®

AuthorHouse™ UK
1663 Liberty Drive
Bloomington, IN 47403 USA
www.authorhouse.co.uk
Phone: 0800.197.4150

Published by AuthorHouse   07/28/2016

ISBN: 978-1-5246-3596-1 (sc)
ISBN: 978-1-5246-3597-8 (hc)
ISBN: 978-1-5246-3598-5 (e)

Print information available on the last page.

This book is dedicated to my mum and dad. Thank you for always talking about Tanzania as I grew up and encouraging me to travel. Also thank you for supporting me and pushing me to be the independent woman I have become. Thanks to you both I listen and live from my heart.

When I decided to do a solo trip to Africa I knew that I would be experiencing a whole new world and I also know how quickly we forget the little details. I didn't want to forget anything I would see, feel and experience on this journey and so I decided to keep a journal of my trip. It began as just something for me and I did it only for me but on the return of my trip and when I started to type it up for myself I thought it would be a lovely story to share. After some encouragement from friends, this personal reflection became a book. I hope it will inspire others to chase their dreams, seek to help others and see how lucky we are.

I want to say a massive thank you to Brijan Barten for encouraging me to do this, for being my support not just through this whole experience but every day. Also thank you to everyone who supported me, donated to the cause and helped me along the way. Also to the volunteer doctors who spare their time to go and help those who really need it. You have no idea just how amazing you are.

One

26th November 2015 15.00

So here I am sitting on a window ledge at Malaga Airport listening to Brijan singing "To make you feel my love' on my phone. I am feeling pretty emotional right now.

When Brijan and I were sitting last night and he suggested loading some songs onto my phone for me to listen to; including one of him singing; I thought it was such a sweet and thoughtful thing to do.

Before I got on the bus for the airport Brijan and I shared a massive hug and letting him go was so hard. I wanted to stay there in his arms where I always feel safe. I feel pathetic when I see that in writing but I suppose we can't help the way we feel.

When we let go he said "There are a few songs of me singing on your phone, so at least you will be able to hear my voice". That means so much to me and truly the loveliest thing anyone has ever done for me. So with hearing that I had to quickly say I love you (while my voice was still able to produce words) and rush onto the bus because tears were clouding my vision and I didn't want him to see them spill down my face.

Once on the bus though, they cascaded down my face. I then of course grabbed my phone to see what he had loaded onto it. There

1

were plenty of lovely songs both by him and other artists, but 'to make you feel my love' came on first and to hear his voice and singing those words were a true comfort to me…. Though it did of course set me off in tears again and it took all the way to the airport for me to get my blubbery mess under control.

So I sit here by the window watching people stroll through departures and see the sun shining through the windows as the planes sit waiting for their passengers. My flight will take me to Edinburgh. I will have a few days with some family and then the real reason I am travelling and the big journey begins; I will be headed to Tanzania.

My emotions and feelings are all over the place and this trip to Tanzania, Africa is why.

When you decide to step out of your comfort zone it can really make you look closer at your life and the people around you. The last few months; and even more so this last week, I have seen just how amazing my life is now and how incredible the people I hold close to me are. I am so lucky and I feel so privileged but I am so scared of going and losing it all. The world is a crazy place just now and so much crap is happening that as much as I am excited I am also starting to feel the nerves and a bit if fear starting to catch up.

I am by no means having second thoughts about going and I would never let the idiots of this world that are trying to scare everyone stop me from living my life and doing the things I want however it is a bit daunting and I hope that all those I love know just how much I love them and how much they really mean to me.

Two

The whole idea of this trip takes us back to the 9th March of this year when I had been chatting to my friend back in Scotland. She was doing her Duke of Edinburgh Award and part of it she had the opportunity to go with people from her company to The Gambia in Africa to do volunteer work. She told me how they can arrange for family or friends to accompany them. I totally jumped at the chance. It was something I had always fancied doing. Here was a great opportunity and to do it with a friend and a group of others would be amazing.

That day my friend sent me an email with more information about the trip and what it would entail and what would be expected of us. It all sounded pretty great to me.

We were asked to raise a certain amount of money (as a minimum) this would cover our accommodation and food in The Gambia and help fund the project.

Everyone would meet the night before we were due to fly out at a hotel by Birmingham Airport so we could have a briefing and a chance to get to know one another before heading on our flight.

I contacted the woman in charge to make sure the fact that I actually reside in Spain wouldn't be an issue (which it wasn't).

Within a few weeks I was signed up and I had already begun organizing fundraising events and coming up with ideas to raise money. I was super excited and had paid the deposit for the trip straight away.

The first big thing I did to raise money and kick of my fundraising campaign was to walk 'The Camanito Del Rey'. This is a narrow walk path along a cliff edge that passes over a gorge and rapid waters in Spain.

Now heights and I have never exactly been the best of friends. It has been one of my massive fears (and brought plenty of amusement to those around me). However when raising money I believe you have to challenge yourself, step out of your comfort zone and really push your limits.

So my best friend Charlotte (who is like a sister to me) and I signed up to go in May (when it was reopening after being closed due to a few deaths and some refurbishment took place) and it did worry me a bit that you had to sign up and give ID numbers to do it, doesn't sound very promising.

Anyway, before I knew it, it was the day of the big walk. People had been sponsoring me both in person and via my fundraising page, so there was no backing out. I was shaking and felt sick as I got up at ridiculous o'clock to get ready. I went and picked up Charlotte who was also a bit nervous. We had a 2 hour drive to get to the Camanito Del Rey and as we approached the nerves were getting worse.

We had our boys 'The New Jersey Boys' album playing which was a comfort for us and helped us relax a little. We drove up singing (badly and out of tune) all the way to the entrance. We were a tad late as we got a little lost at one point as there is a section not signposted). We were nervous they wouldn't let us in late which would be a disaster. People were expecting us to do this and we had psyched ourselves up and were so determined to succeed. So we got to the front of the little que and thankfully there were no problems. We were handed a hard hat (again not exactly reassuring – and also can't help but think that it wouldn't really do much should I actually fall off a cliff edge) and told to wait. Oh the nerves were really going crazy now, we were trying to be brave but our faces couldn't disguise how we were really feeling.

The first 5 to 10 minutes of the walk are easy and you start to feel a false sense of security. Then you get to the top of a wee hill and you see where you are about to walk and the wee bridge going from one cliff to the other over rapid water. I am sure my heart stopped beating for a minute before starting again at an unbelievably ridiculous rate.

Charlotte reassured me and we continued (at a more reluctant pace). Then we got to the entrance to the tiny path. You had to sign in before stepping through a gate and onto the so called "path". Lets just say from word go I wasn't exactly a big fan. You see the thing is this "walkway" was basically wooden planks and there were gaps. As if walking a cliff edge wasn't bad enough, some genius thought lets add insult to injury and make the steps far apart and tiny so you have to look down to step up and you can't miss seeing through the massive gap. People warn you not to look down when trying to deal with heights – well whoever designed the path was obviously having a chuckle to themselves when they made it an impossibility. You encounter all this within 10 minutes of starting. Then before you know it you have to go over the bridge.

Well they call it a bridge; I saw it as more of a death trap. I was most definitely not up for it. This 'bridge' was thin metal that swung, more like a rope bridge. Again the evil architect must have thought that's not scary enough, why don't we put holes in the sheets of metal so everyone sees right down, to the rapid water passing by all that way down there. A big warning bell went off in my head when I see a sign just before crossing warning only a maximum of 8 people on the bridge at any given time. Now 8 people is not a lot and to me there having to be a limit screams that it is not very stable.

So Charlotte and I had to let someone go ahead of us as little me needed to build up the courage to go across, much to the amusement of some people waiting to cross. I can't say anyones reaction or opinion was really a concern nor did it really register.

I was going at a snails pace and I had a death grip on the edge of the wires going across. I made it though, thanks to Charlotte encouraging me as we went across. After that the walk wasn't so bad (though the plaque dedicated to the 3 people who died walking the Camanito Del Rey was not what you would call a comfort) and the more we walked the more relaxed I got. Charlotte chatting to me kept me distracted and soon we were off the cliff walking on solid ground. We sung Jersey Boys songs, had a wee giggle and a spot of our packed lunches.

We made it to the other side and it felt great but it is not one way so we had to turn and face it all again going back' having made it that way in amazing time. The way back wasn't too bad, but as we were getting closer to the bridge of doom, I grew quieter and quieter. My fear was starting to get the better of me again. Bless my fab sister was talking about all sorts of rubbish to keep me distracted (including vacuum seal packaging).

The second crossing of the bridge was no easier than the first. In fact if possible it was worse. There were people going in both directions now and trying to pass me, I really didn't like that. Charlotte thought this was a great photo opportunity, can't say I was of the same opinion. At least I could provide a laugh for those around me.

We finally got to the end and the relief I felt was crazy. I was a bit emotional but so proud that we had done it and so thankful to have my sister by my side.

Me taking on the Camanito Del Rey

Three

Sunday 29th November 2015

So I have had a few days in Edinburgh, giving me a chance to spend time with my brother, sister in law and baby niece (oh and their dog of course).

It has given me a chance to sort out the last of the Christmas presents, pop into my brother's tattoo studio, go for walks with my sister in law, baby niece and their dog, watched some old home movies and get myself prepared for my trip.

So I wake this morning (thanks for the message at 7.30am Mum – and thanks to me for giving my mum the ringtone 'your mum is calling back' to the song 'I'm bringing sexy back') to an email from Lisa (the woman helping me organize going over to do the volunteer work).

So it turns out that there has been a cholera outbreak at the hospital where I am supposed to be going, and I have also learnt that it was at the hospital that I was to be staying, so Lisa and I have been emailing back and forth as we try to work out what we are going to do. 30 people have been infected within 24 hours so it is really bad. It is no longer possible to stay at the hospital and although I have taken oral vaccines against cholera I am still at risk.

It is so bad the government have sent people up to help in the hospital with a medical background. So now things have to be played by ear as to when I can go up and how long I can stay there and to what it is possible for me to do in order to help while I am there. It is all quite daunting to be on my way to Africa and no longer know where I can stay or what I will be doing and knowing going up will put me at great risk of getting ill.

Time to make some kind of a plan B.

Four

The amount of support I received for doing the Camanito Del Rey was a wonderful surprise. I had some unbelievably generous donations but every penny donated has an impact, no matter how small. There were so many people that got behind me and went out their way to help.

I was so happy with how it was going but there was still so much more to be done and I was determined to reach my goals.

I started to think about the little things I could do throughout the summer (a difficult time for me to do anything as I work crazy amounts as it is seasonal work here on the sunny coast of Spain) and I was starting to brainstorm about hosting a charity night.

I work in a bar – venue sorted, 3 of my closest friends are singers – entertainment sorted and with the help and support of my sis I had everything I would need. So I spoke to the people concerned and thankfully they were all happy to help me.

I booked the 14th November at the bar I work in called Legends, the boys agreed to do their 'New Jersey Boys' tribute as well as the 'Blues Brothers' tribute, some swing music to start the night and to end the night with some upbeat songs to dance to.

I spoke with Charlotte and she was up for dancing but was more nervous about doing anything too upbeat, which is what I had in mind for one of the dances, so she suggested I dance with Brijan as he is a great dancer. I put the idea across to Brijan and to my relief he was totally up for it but he had something slightly different in mind.

Before I got the chance to do anything more the woman organizing the trip and my friend were in touch. It looked like things were on the line for the trip. After a week of emails going back and forth it was confirmed they had indeed cancelled the trip. I was absolutely gutted as I had raised so much money already and I had it in my head I was doing this.

So with arrangements in place to get my deposit back from the charity, I looked into other charities. But again this thought of "you must raise X amount" kept niggling in my head. I was chatting to my mum about it and I told her I was thinking of heading somewhere solo.

I am sure to nobody's surprise; my mum was not keen on the idea. She asked me to hold on a few days; maybe she could contact an old friend from her days in Tanzania.

You see back before my brother and I were born my parents lived in Tanzania for a few years (I believe it was 1982 to 1987) and a couple of their friends were still residing there.

My mum soon got back to me with an email address for a woman called Lisa. Lisa told me about an organization set up in a village called Beta, where they had set up and were running a Hospital, School and Orphanage. She told me of their struggles for supplies, vaccines, support and I was offering straight away to get involved.

So things were set in motion. I would go over, do some volunteer work and most importantly help raise money to help them out.

As soon as it was confirmed I was straight online to book my flights. I was so desperate to get organized I even used my lunch break at the beach (where I am a masseuse) to sit and book my tickets as soon as I had confirmed I would go.

But with it all booked and everything getting organized, I was even more driven to raise as much money as possible.

Five

So I am on board the Etihad flight to Abu Dhabi. It is all really happening!

I don't seem to feel nervous anymore, just super excited. Though I am sure once I am on the flight to Dar Es Salam the nerves will kick back in.

So yesterday the whole cholera epedemic came to light and I am still having to play things by ear, however I feel relaxed about it as I have booked a hotel in Dar for the whole time I was supposed to be in Beta, so if we can't stay up there (which appears to be the case so far) I am not all of a sudden stranded in Tanzania with nowhere to stay.

Lisa and I will go pick up a load of medicine from the Pharmacy to help with the cholera outbreak (the money I have raised will be used straight away to assist a real life problem) and to restock the hospital with medicines and supplies they are in desperate need of. It seems to make sense to spend the money on this when the problem is happening right now and that's the urgent neccessity. We will travel up to Beta together to get these much needed supplies to them but how long we can stay and how much I can do to assist will all depend on how bad things are. I don't want

15

to be in the way and put ourselves or others at high risk. We will just have to wait and see what happens.

So it was up at 3 this morning to get ready for the airport. Showered, breakfast, washing on etc. Then picked up by the taxi at 5.15am (which I had to stand outside and wait for as the buzzer to the flat is broken and my Spanish number won't work in the UK).

It was the weirdest thing, but as I approached the airport the song Begging came on the radio. This is one of the songs my sis and I dance to as the Jersey Girls and the one we were dancing to when we did the Camanito Del Rey. It was a comfort to hear the song and I felt it was a positive sign and put a massive grin across my face. It was like my friends were there encouraging and supporting me.

Check-in was quick and easy (couldn't get checked in online – that was a whole other drama yesterday) and before I knew it I was sitting outside gate 11 at Edinburgh Airport sipping a small hot chocolate from Costa.

I had already popped into Superdrug to stock up a little more on hand sanitizer with this whole cholera epedemic.

Once on board I was so happy to have two seats to myself. Feet up and relaxed. I watched 'The Minions Movie' which I enjoyed and I plan to read a bit of my book next.

I have a 12 hour lay over in Abu Dhabi, so my parents are driving over from Dubai (where they live) to see me. As it is overnight we are booked into the airport hotel, so we get a chance of a bit of sleep. It will be so great to see them before the big trip.

Six

Over the summer I did the odd thing here and there (doing specials with my hair and beauty business with a certain amount going to my charity).

Brijan and I started our dancing rehearsals near the end of the summer. The dance Brijan had suggested (and to begin with I thought was a joke) was none other than 'Time of your life' from Dirty Dancing. We decided to keep it a secret, making it a surprise on the night.

We mixed our rehearsals between lifts and the actual dance routine. Charlotte and Ben let us use the pool on their complex to do our first couple lift rehearsals. We had such a laugh doing it. We decided to record it because we were laughing so much and so many funny things happened.

The first time Brijan went to pick me up I was pretty nervous, as was he. We giggled so much and had a great time during our rehearsals (probably laughed more than we lifted). When we felt comfortable enough in the pool (which was only after three times) we moved onto the beach to practice on the sand before we did it on solid ground. Actually looking back I am surprised we hadn't done more rehearsals, it felt like so much more than it was. But it was great fun.

Brijan and I practicing "The Lift" on the beach in La Cala

Brijan had tweaked the original dance as obviously doing it live is different to on screen. So he taught me all the moves and I recorded each bit at a time as he taught me so I could practice when Brijan wasn't around. I would walk the boardwalk along the beach at night with my phone and headphones watching the video and doing some of the steps. My dancing abilities are nowhere near Brijan's, so I had a lot more work to do. But he remained patient throughout the whole process and always encouraged me.

Seven

Tuesday 1st December 2015 09:00 AD / 08:00 TNZ

So that is the plane taken off and I am on my way to Tanzania! Oh my god this is so surreal. Well there is no turning back now.

Last night I was pleasantly surprised to see Abu Dhabi airport has had a massive upgrade and makeover since I was last there. That will be good on my 6 hour wait on the way back. I was straight up to passport control and it didn't take long for my bag to come through on the conveyer belt and I was soon walking through the arrivals door to see my parents standing there waiting for me.

It was great to see them both. We were booked into the Premier Inn which is a 2 minute walk through a little crossing, where you walk past a McDonalds, a Pharmacy, O'Briens, a Spa (both a men's and ladies') to name but a few. We stopped at McDonalds for something to eat. We had a right laugh as my dad has a print out from McDonalds showing exactly how he likes his burger (bun, burger, cheese, onion and tomato – nothing else) that he now hands over at the till when he makes an order (he does make me giggle). We were of course chatting away about my trip ahead.

We then went to our room (where my mum freaked out at me re-hooking the curtains she had accidently pulled down – she thought I would lean on the window and then it would suddenly break). I went about re-organising my bags while dad called room service and ordered us a drink.

During this time I received an email with the full list of supplies and medicine that had been ordered from the Pharmacy for Beta. I let them know how much money was available and they could make an order equal to the amount I had raised. So Isaac put an order in to the supplier in Dar Es Salaam and they would deliver it to Beta. The hospital are in desperate need of so much. Attached to the email was a receipt and full list of all that was bought and the quantities bought.

As I read through the list and quantities I was shocked and proud, not to mention excited at how much the money was supplying for the hospital; even more so at such a time of need for them. I really am so thrilled. It is the most rewarding feeling to know how much of a difference we had made. All the hard work people put in and all the kind donations – I was seeing the actual real life results!

So we all sat and marveled over this amazing news and chatted about what was to come. Then it was time for lights out and to try and get some rest.

At 6am this morning the alarm went off and my body wasn't ready to get up but I was soon wide awake as my mind raced at what lay ahead. So it was a quick shower and ready for the flight. Mum and dad walked me to the terminal where Etihad was crazy busy. Thankfully we were put in a short queue (but moved at an incredibly slow speed) where I checked in my small trolley weighing 12kg, certainly travelling light!

Then it was massive hugs as I said bye to dad and mum (who was all choked up) and I promised to get in contact as soon as I possibly could. I have no idea what I am going to, so who knows when I will get the chance.

I was then on my own and headed to passport control. This is when I was expecting the nerves to really kick in but I felt strangely calm and at ease. The queue for passport control took forever and by the time I got through I was rushing off to my gate (very quickly buying a Caesar wrap to take on board as I hadn't eaten yet; and I don't like plane food). I got to the gate and quickly joined the end of a short queue as they changed the status to last call.

I was on board in a few minutes and at the back of the plane, minus one row.

I was glad when only one person joined and we had the middle seat free, giving us plenty of room. A smooth take off and now I am en route to Dar Es Salaam. Now it is time for me to eat my chicken wrap. So excited about what lies ahead!

Eight

The owners of the bar that I work at announced that they were to close in November for refurbishment, meaning they would be closed when I was due to have my charity event there. They offered to do it in October instead but that didn't work for the boys, and I really needed them for the entertainment and it wouldn't be the same without them. I then had to set about finding a new venue.

I decided if I wasn't able to have it at Legends, then I didn't want to use another bar. I decided to do it at a restaurant, with a dinner and show. Turn it into a more of a ball. I believe everything happens for a reason and I think it was meant to be a ball.

I went a few places to enquire about the event, some took too long to get back to me, some just weren't right and then there was one that didn't even bother to turn up to our meeting then got a waiter to call me and asked to do it over the phone (their loss in the end). Then I thought about the restaurant that sits behind me where I am set up doing massage on the beach. The food is great and I know the owner (though it was the owner that put me off wanting to go to there). So I went and spoke to him and he recommended using his other restaurant called El Capricho in Calahonda (10 minute drive from me). He took me down to see it and it was a great location and the setting was just right for what I was looking for. So we agreed on a price, date and time.

One of my friends who does an act here had agreed to co-host the night with me and also said he would design the poster for me so we met up to go over what needed to go on the poster. I then went home to design and order the tickets for the night.

A few days after that I got the design through from my friend and I sent it to the printers to get some printed and laminated. I know them in there and they did them for me in a couple days.

Once the tickets arrived the posters were put up and I started to advertise the night on Facebook and twitter. Whenever I spoke to anyone I would let them know about the night too. I was still working 7 hours on the beach doing massage and working at Legends at night. I didn't really think about how much work had to be done during my busy season. Although the ball wasn't till the 7th November a lot of the leg work had to happen while I was still busy.

Then I got a message from my friend saying he had accidently double booked the night and he actually had another gig to do. I couldn't believe it. At first I panicked a little but not for long. I know enough people and people like to help when it comes to charity. For some reason a friend of mine Mike (Michael Nunan) came into my head. I could just see him being perfect for the job. Mike and I hadn't spent that much time together but I really hoped he would help me out.

So I sent him a message explaining exactly what I was doing and what I was asking of him. He said he would love to help and suggested meeting for a coffee so we could go over things.

While this was happening I got an email with an update of the poster, removing my friends name from it (as that is false advertisement) and I sent them off to the printers.

Things were a little stressful but no knockback had knocked me down.

Nine

1st December 2015 19:00

So I am in Tanzania! I can't really believe I am finally here. I had a decent flight and as I came into land I had 'The Lion King' soundtrack playing as I promised my brother I would. It was so exciting seeing Tanzania below as we came in to land. To see how different the areas were. From built up areas to sparse land. Upon arrival a fire engine sprayed us with water, at first I didn't understand why but I thought it was pretty cool.

Then when we were exited from the rear of the plane it was apparent someone important was on board as there was a red carpet laid out in front of the front exit and loads of people were gathered as well as people dressed up on stilts and music was being played. It was so magnificent to see.

We were put on a wee bus that drives 30 seconds to the airport door (it really could be walked). The airport is tiny and very old school. You walk through the door and there are some dark brown cubicles on the right. You go here and they take your passport and visa application (this was given to you on the flight). You have your picture taken by a wee camera and a machine takes all your fingerprints (ok this part isn't old school but in general it looks it). Then you have to pay your visa (50 USD – price depends on where you are from and your purpose of visit). They then take everything and hand it to some guys in a little windowed office and you have to stand and wait just further on from the desks.

They take their time and the waiting area gets busier but no passports are coming back (gets a bit nerve-wracking). Then suddenly 6 came at once. They read out your name and you are handed back your passport and directed to passport control (which you can't miss as it is two steps ahead of you and the only direction you can go other than back onto the runway). They wave you through passport control and you are straight on top of the luggage. My bag came out a few seconds after I got there and a few steps to your right is the x-ray machines to put your bags through then you are at the exit.

I was glad to see very quickly the guy holding a sign with my name on it (although it was upside down haha). He was such a friendly guy and chatted to me on the way to the hotel. His name was Sardeh and he told me he had two daughters but wanted many more children and he hoped that one would be a boy.

I was still feeling relaxed and I couldn't take enough in as we drove to the hotel. I loved seeing the guys selling things at the traffic lights. I mean everything from full length mirrors to ice-cream to shirts to sling shots! It was so incredible.

Sardeh told me I was to be very careful by the hotel as it wasn't the best area. He asked me why I was staying there and told me I shouldn't be in that area. As we got closer to the hotel I could see what he meant. It was more run down than what we had been driving through and we were now on a beaten track dirt road rather than a tarmac road.

I had a warm greeting at the hotel and Joyce got me checked in. I was helped up to my room with my bags as the lift was broken and I was on the fifth floor. I got myself semi-organised and popped downstairs to get a drink. I felt so dehydrated. When I got downstairs (5 floors to walk down) the woman informed me I had to pay in Tanzanian shillings (I had assumed it would be in USD as everything had been quoted to me in USD. You can't get Tanzanian shillings outside Tanzania). I was directed to a bureau de change where I exchanged some money. I got back and bought some water and a Fanta (after using the lobby wifi to send an I am safe message to Brijan and my family while I waited for Joyce to finish her meal). Then up to my room where I guzzled down the Fanta.

I had also messaged Lisa to find out what the plan was for tomorrow. But I would have to pop up and down five floors to check with the wifi. Also I wanted to explore. I was too excited to stay locked up in my room. So I thought I would go explore a little and buy a sim card. So I headed back down the five floors and asked Joyce where I could buy a sim. She told me I was "too sweet to go alone" and they could help me.

She informed me that I would need a copy of my passport and she would do it for me as it isn't safe to get it done outside. So back up the five flights I went to go and get my passport and then back down again where Joyce copied it for me and called the concierge/security guy to go with me to buy a sim.

Literally at the street corner of the hotel sat a woman at a plastic garden table with a big garden umbrella on the street selling sim cards. A first for me. So we bartered a price and I had a sim for my phone. I was a little uneasy and I realized I was not in an area to go exploring alone. So I went straight back to the hotel with the concierge. I went to get my passport off Joyce (who kindly agreed to take care of it while I went and got my sim); and she requested I pay the airport transfer fare (something I had assumed would be done at check out as it hadn't been mentioned during check-in). So up and down five flights again to get the USD that the fare had to be paid in (not allowed to pay the airport transfer in shillings for some reason) but I would need to wait for my change as she didn't have any. Then finally back up the five flights where I would now chill.

I got my mosquito net up, had a few biscuits and got the TV on. Now I have written this and I plan on an early night. I am shattered.

Ten

Mike and I met for coffee and he asked me lots of questions and really went through what I was doing, not just on the night but before and after. Why I wanted to help the organization, what the plans were, how I had raised money so far etc. I hadn't expected all that but it made me feel like he was the one that was supposed to host with me. He really cared about what I was doing and interested about the whole thing. He took it on to be as personal to him as it is to me. That means a lot to me.

It ended up being a really good season and I was working on the beach till the end of October (great for me) but meant squeezing in rehearsals around work. Dance rehearsals with Brijan were in full swing as were my rehearsals with Charlotte.

Charlotte and I were doing two dances. One to 'All that jazz' and one to a 60s melody. I had choreographed both of these dances and taught them to Charlotte. So we were trying to rehearse where possible too.

It was a lot of work but it was also so much fun. We had a good laugh doing it all and we thoroughly enjoyed it. What more can you ask for really.

Tickets were selling and I got donations before the night from people that knew what I was doing but couldn't make the night. The support I was getting from everyone, especially my friends was more than anyone could dream.

Eleven

1st December 2015 22:10

So I started to drift off quite quickly after I finished writing only to get a call from reception at 8.30pm to say they finally had my change from paying the airport transfer fare, could I come down and get it. So down the five flights I went to pick up my change. Straight back into bed and I was into a sleep quite quick. Then about twenty minutes later there was a thudding at my door and I woke with shock. It didn't stop so I quickly and quietly ran to the door to see through the peephole what was going on. A man stood there. I was a little panicked but was so relieved when the room opposite opened their door and the man, it would appear, had the wrong room number. It did give me a fright though and although I have calmed down, I feel very much awake and alert now.

Twelve

We had some great laughs doing our dance rehearsals. Brijan and I were often giggling away and I was often in hysterical laughter. The thing with me though is once I get the giggles I find it so hard to stop laughing and when I am with Brijan we are always having a great time and he really makes me laugh and we always have a fun together.

There were several things that gave us the giggles during rehearsals. When we were practicing the lift at the beginning one of the things we laughed about a lot was I would run to jump then wimp out and turn and run back then when Brijan went to lift me but he knew he hadn't got it he would put me down saying "No No No No" (kind of like the guy from the tv series The Vicar of Dibley). To begin with Brijan wasn't so gentle and setting me back down, he would almost throw me to the ground, especially if he was frustrated because he hadn't got it right. We had a good chuckle over it.

I also gained a new nickname from Brijan during rehearsals and that was finger monkey. When we were beginning out with the lifts and Brijan lifted me and I thought I might fall I would wrap my legs and arms around him so I wouldn't fall and hold onto him. He laughed so hard and said I was like a finger monkey and that became his wee name for me during our rehearsals. Between Brijan throwing me down, me wrapping myself around him, the wedgies I sometimes got when he grabbed my bikini bottoms (not to mention the one time one side of my bikini bottoms came undone as he put me down and they nearly totally fell off – but I am sure nobody saw that, and of course my bikini top came down a few times when we had started lifts in the pool) I am sure we must have been some sight for anyone watching us at the beginning of our rehearsals.

Then there were the injuries that came into play (but still made us laugh). From where Brijan was holding me and lifting me up by my hip bones I had bruises from his thumbs digging into me. Not the nicest thing and painful having thumbs digging into your bruises but I would be so caught up in the lifts and laughter I would forget again till the next day when I woke up. I was also still having to take care when dancing as in the June I partially tore the ligament in my knee when doing backing dancing for a band here at the Salon Varities Theatre in Fuengirola.

When we were getting a step forward we would get excited and high five both of us often forgetting I had a cut hand and that hurt like hell. So here I should give you a bit of a back story.

So one evening I had a night off work at the bar (I only have one night off a week) and I was chilling out and fancied cooking myself a Scottish breakfast for dinner. So I got the tattie scones and square sausage out the freezer and bacon out the fridge. So I was separating the sausages with the pointy knife when it hit an air pocket in the sausage and suddenly the knife went straight through and into my hand. Now it went quite deep and started bleeding profusely. I started to feel light headed and panicked a little thinking in my head that if I fainted and hit my head nobody would even know till I didn't pitch up at the beach the next morning. So I made my way to the sofa thinking if I pass out there at least I am safe. I managed to grab my phone as I made my way to lie down while clutching a tea towel to my wound trying to get the bleeding to stop. As I made it to the sofa and lay down I tucked my right hand under my left side using that to put pressure on my hand as I typed a message to Brijan – "Accidently stabbed myself but think I am OK".

Admittedly a stupid thing to write as it sounds really bad and poor Brijan thought there was something seriously wrong as I lay there trying to keep myself awake and get the bleeding to stop. As it subsided and my head became less fuzzy and I could focus I saw the messages from Brijan saying oh my god and are you ok, what happened. I slowly got up and made my way to the kitchen. Got myself a wee drink of water and a bite of chocolate for sugar and messaged back saying it was just my hand and I was totally ok and then carried on cooking my dinner.

It was also really hard to keep the dance we were doing under wraps. A lot of people were asking me what we would be doing and trying to rehearse on the beach without people we knew seeing us wasn't easy.

One day we were practicing and the weather had been lovely so several people had been out walking and quite a few people were watching us as we were trying to get our lift right. At first I thought people watching us would make me too nervous and embarrassed but I was so focused and determined (and having too much fun with Brijan) to pay much attention to anyone else. Then two men walked passed us and joked asking if they were getting picked up next. The weather turned and as the rain began we decided to head home, bumping into the two men again who joked they were just heading back to pick me up. That evening as I was working in Legends the same two men walked in and asked me how the lifting had gone and was it for a dance. I had to quickly hush them and explain that it was a surprise for my charity event. Sure to say if we ever mentioned lifts people would guess the dance we had planned.

Thirteen

2nd December 2015 18:00

So last night I think someone was having a laugh, as I finally started to drift off when the room phone rang. Again I woke with a jump and it turned out to be the wrong room (someone was obviously giving out the wrong room number). Between the two calls and the man banging on my door it had been an eventful night. So needless to say I didn't get the best night's sleep, but it wasn't too bad either.

This morning I was up by 7am. There isn't exactly what you would call a shower in the hotel room, so I decided to use wet wipes to give myself a wash. I got ready and carried my stuff down (yes those five flights of stairs again) to the lobby. I sent my mum a quick message to let her know that I had survived the night and then went and got in a taxi to take me to 50 Mirambo Street where I was to meet Lisa.

I was given the British Council as a reference point. Lisa told me to leave an hour before our meeting time of 9am as it would take that amount of time due to traffic. I had google mapped it though and it said it was only 8 minutes away but traffic yesterday showed me things can be pretty crazy, so I decided to leave at 8.20am.

The taxi driver took me to the British Council (as that was on the piece of paper I handed him) and refused to stop at number 50 as that wasn't the British Council. So I was dropped off and had to walk back down the street with my bags while calling Lisa. I had got there in just 15 minutes and so I wanted her know I was there already. However she told me I was early and she wasn't there yet. So I stood on the opposite side of the road to her gated building, against a concrete block at the side of the British Council.

All of a sudden a peacock just appeared wondering down the road. I was shocked and absolutely loved it. I really wanted to take a photo but you are not allowed to take photos by consulates. It was so surreal and I felt like I really was in Africa.

At just after 9am Lisa arrived and signed me into the building. First she took me to the car so I could leave my bags then up to her husband Steve's office, where I got to meet him. We then went to Lisa's office; a storage room on the roof (fully air-conditioned) where she had massive boxes of knitted jumpers and hats that people all over the world have made and sent to her charity 'Knitz', where she then gets them to kids across Tanzania that desperately need them. During winter some places can get awfully cold and so many children die of hypothermia or pneumonia (we are so lucky to have heating and warm clothing). They need to be sorted, logged, bagged and tagged before they are sent out to those in need.

First we headed to the Sheraton Hotel with all my euros to convert them into Tanzanian Shillings. We had a coffee (well a water for me – I don't drink coffee) then back to the office. So I helped Lisa pair jumpers with hats and log them, bag them in 100s and, tag them and ready them for their destination. We bagged up 600 for 0-3 year olds and 100 for 3-6 year olds. During the process of it all we had a little break to go down and pay the man for all the medical supplies being delivered to Beta Hospital. Once the money was all counted, Steve took us out for a drink (I was boring and had water again haha).

So when we had filled and totally packed up the car with bags of knitted wear for the kids we drove over to Oyster Bay, taking a longer route through Upanga so I could see places and areas my parents would have known from their time in Dar.

We went to a café called Black Tomato at Oyster Bay, before we went to a supermarket called Food Lovers. We bought some food for our trip up to Beta (where we would have nowhere to buy food and the few things available you have to be wary of due to the cholera outbreak).

We squeezed these into the few gaps available in the car. Then we went to Lisa's where I waited for my taxi man to come to take me to my new hotel. Suker the taxi man was a chatty man from the minute I got in. I judge him to be about ages with me. He welcomed me to Tanzania and chatted to me about everything from his baby boy (Daniel) who is just 8 months, to how his taxi service work works, about the new president (who is helping to crush out the corruption), education and how I need to come back many times to Tanzania. He was a lovely man and so happy.

When I arrived at the hotel (Ledger Bahari Beach) I was pleasantly surprised. I was greeted with a mango juice, promptly checked in and taken to my hotel room. Even walking through the outside I knew this was a massive improvement on my last hotel. There are separate buildings like little cottages (four rooms to a cottage). I was up the stairs and I was well surprised at how lovely the room is. It is so nice and I realized what a great deal I got. I had paid so little for the five nights.

I quickly skyped my mum (yay there was wifi in the room) then went for a little exploration. I walked down onto the beach (which I have a view of from my room), walked by the pool and then went to my room to have a proper shower! It felt really good. Now I am going to unpack and chill.

Ledger Bahari Beach

Fourteen

The week leading up to the Beta Ball was a busy one. Dance rehearsals were now a daily thing (thanks to Legends for letting us use the space to rehearse). I was dropping off last minute ticket sales and trying to draw up the table plan. I went to buy table centers (as the restaurant didn't have any) and for table numbers I bought wooden numbers and spray painted them black and sprinkled gold glitter over them. I also bought the prop plastic guns Charlotte and I need for in our 'all that jazz' dance routine. I could only get one black and one silver so I spray painted the silver one black too. I also had to ensure we all had what we needed for costume changes for all the dances.

I had to get all the music transferred onto USB sticks and make up a playlist for background music for when the live entertainment was not on.

Then there was collecting all the prizes that had been kindly donated for the raffle. There were many wonderful donations from Sai Indian Restaurant, Forever Living, Wags and Lads Boutique, Something Different, Julie Jane – Hair, Beauty and Massage, Miss Fit Marbella, Las Casitas, Bottle hampers from Chris and Alan, flowers and chocolates from Jenny and Gerry.

Fifteen

3rd December 2015 08:30

So I woke up at 5.30 this morning after an amazing night's sleep. I got my bag packed for going up to Beta and was happy my tops I had hand washed at the sink last night were dry.

At 06:40 I went for breakfast as it opens from 06:20. It was completely empty and I had to find a waiter to sign in and the buffet was half empty but there was enough out for me to get a decent enough breakfast. As the directory says the pool opens at 7am I thought I would get a little swim in but when I got down there the security guy told me that it didn't open until 8am. Disappointed I went back to the room and picked up some euros I wanted to exchange and headed to reception, where I was told I couldn't get anything exchanged until 8am (not what it says in the directory either). So I went back to my room and got myself showered and ready.

I popped back to reception at 8am and got the money exchanged and now I am chilling till Lisa comes at 9am.

3rd December 2015 21:12

Lisa arrived early this morning at 8.35 which was great as I was ready to go. I met her at the restaurant and we headed off for Beta. We chatted away as we started the long drive to Beta. We started to get to know each other and discussed the trip ahead of us and what it would be like at Beta and what I hoped to carry on doing for them.

We stopped about 2 hours into the drive when Lisa worried we had taken a wrong turn (or missed it to be precise) but decided to carry on after speaking to Steve, then we pulled through a petrol station to quickly check we were headed in the right direction.

Then we carried on driving for quite a while before a quick toilet stop. Well that was an experience as it is a hole on the floor as opposed to an actual toilet (been there before) and there is a woman casually wandering around in her underwear as she is doing a load of washing at the grubby sinks.

As we continued to drive Lisa was pulled over at one point by the police for speeding. She was fighting with them in Swahili and then she just said she refused to pay a fine as it is ridiculous and she drove off! Yes that is correct; she just drove off away from the police. I was shocked, but what shocked me more was the police did nothing about it!

The driving here is definitely worth a mention. I thought I had seen bad driving; I mean they aren't the best in Spain and in Saudi Arabia, Bahrain and Dubai they are a bit nuts and drive way too fast but here they are a whole other kettle of fish.

You have lorries and big buses trying to overtake other lorries and big buses on the wrong side of the road as they are going over a steep hill, where you can't see what is coming over the other side. It is madness. Then you have the guys on motorbikes who clearly don't even have a license and they are loaded up with an unbelievable amount. I have no idea how they balance and they can't always and you see them tip on the road…. Poor guys.

Then the lorries who don't know how to drive properly either and end up tipped over in a ditch. Also over here most don't have a red triangle to indicate an accident so they put down broken branches on the road or side of the road to indicate trouble ahead. It is so unreal to see.

We drove to Morogoro (all in all about 5 ½ hours driving) where we stopped to have our lunch. Then it was on to Beta Village (about another hour and a half driving). Morogoro was already a lot more run down and basic compared to Dar but as we got closer to Beta it was getting worse and worse. There are very few concrete buildings, most still live in mud huts. To reach Beta you drive down a beaten dirt track that is totally bumping up and down, then over a wee bridge that looks far from safe (the river bed is also totally dried up). You see all the kids sitting on the dirty ground outside the mud huts, it is a sad sight as you see how dirty they are and so many look like they have almost a grey colour to their skin and just not well.

We got to the wee house we would stay in. We were greeted by a guy called Alistair and a woman called Kristien who stay at the house, later we would meet Emma, Alistair's wife.

Alistair and Kristien welcomed us in and showed us to our rooms. The wee house is simple and basic but there is some electricity and a proper toilet. No working shower but that doesn't bother me. We went through and had a good chat with Alistair and Kristien and then Emma arrived. I found my chats with them really insightful and they have really got me re-thinking how to move forward with my fundraising and what the money should be used for.

They told me how desperate they have been for supplies and medicines and how sparse the hospital is. How basic and lack of proper tools and equipment make things so hard but most of all what there needs to be is an end goal. A plan so at some point they will be self sufficient, and not depending on the likes of me donating and not depending on foreign volunteer doctors like themselves. It truly was a mind opening conversation and I see things in a totally different light.

While sitting Lisa said she was starting to feel a little under the weather and would call it an early night. This gave me a chance to get to chat and know the others a little bit better and ask the questions I really wanted to ask and hear what they had to say and their opinions on things.

Kristien and Alistair went to do rounds at the ward and I chatted away to Emma. I had my Forever Living chocolate meal replacement shake while she told me about what she was doing out here. She is trying to help to get proper sanitation to the village. Then Alistair came running in to grab some of his things as there was an emergency at the hospital. It was quite a thing to witness.

Sixteen

The night before the ball was all about getting things out and ready to go, rehearsals and trying to deal with the nerves building up inside me. I was really starting to crap it.

I was in Legends with Charlotte doing rehearsals in the afternoon, where we let Andrea see the whole routines and listened to her feedback which we were surprised and relieved to hear was so good. This is not our profession and a little out our comfort zone despite thoroughly enjoying doing it.

Then I drove up to Torremolinos to pick up Brijan so we could drive back down to La Cala to do our rehearsals in Legends. I was a little snappy with the poor guy as he was supposed to stay the night at mine but as he wasn't organized I would have drop him off and get him the next day and I was totally panicking that I was having to alter my plans (silly I know but I can admit when I am being unreasonable and stressy) and was so worried he wouldn't get to La Cala in time.

So into Legends we went to do our final rehearsal. Man was I crapping it by this stage and even more so when we finally tried to do the lift in the perfect dress I got for it but we realized that the material was too slippy and he couldn't do the lift with it. Then it was having to think of a plan B. But in the mean time we had to focus on the actual dance. We still had a good laugh and we were in hysterics when we were rehearsing and Briajn came towards me and I went blank and just walked away saying don't worry I won't do this tomorrow. Ooops.

When we finished rehearsing it was getting on into the night, so I drove Brijan back up to Torremolinos and headed back to try and work out how I was going to sort my dress so we wouldn't have a problem with the lift. I was so nervous by now and worried about having everything I couldn't even bare to eat.

I got into my flat and I was brainstorming on what to do with my dress. My original idea was to unpick the top part of the dress from the bottom so it was like a top and skirt, then I could whip the skirt off for the lift with wee shorts on underneath then pop it back on after. But when I looked at the dress and how much work that would be and the fact I am a novice with sewing I thought best not. So instead I decided to alter a body suit I had so I could wear that under the dress with the wee shorts, whip the whole dress off then back on. So I am then panicking about all the sewing I have to do and how we will need to rehearse the dress coming off and on the next day when we are setting up (and ask Charlotte to assist me).

So I get sewing then get all the bags ready with everything in them for the next day and double and checking my list that I have everything. It was about midnight by the time I got into bed and I can assure you it was some time later before I fell asleep.

Seventeen

I woke up this morning at around 6am. Seems to be the routine I have gotten into here. So I got up and drank some water and got my things together to get washed. So I boiled some water and poured it into the big bucket and then added some cool water. Then into the bathroom, stripped off and using a small cup I wet my hair, lathered in the shampoo and a couple cups of water to rinse, then conditioner in and a cup to wet any part of the body that didn't get wet while doing my hair before lathering up with my shower gel and finishing off with tipping what was left in the bucket over me to rinse everything off. It is crazy how little water we actually need to wash and to be honest a bucket shower isn't really that bad.

Then time for breakfast which was another shake and an apple. Kristien was up and told me Lisa had not been well in the night. Lisa had spent the majority of last night being sick and had diahorrea and she is still really bad today. Not a good sign. The doctors we are staying with have been trying to work out what it can be, there are a few possibilities so while Lisa stays in bed and the doctors head off to their morning meeting, Emma has said she will take me around the village.

So I got my camera, sanitizing gel, water and sunglasses and headed out with Emma. We had a good chat and I got some answers to some of my questions about life in the bush. It was surreal to see little huts set up as a hair salon, little bar etc. They were surrounded by mud huts where the people lived. Families would all cram into one hut together and with their animals too (chickens, pigs, goats; whatever it is that they had). These places are so small and that is where they eat, sleep, wash and everything. Though food is usually actually cooked outside. But you can understand why there are so many health problems.

The mud huts they live in

The families are big as they have so many kids so they can be looked after when they are getting older but so many die so very young. The more children they have, the higher the chance some will still be around to care for them in old age. So the basic attitude is have more children so if some die you still have some around. They don't value life in the same way we do in the western world and that is so difficult to digest. It has been a tough lesson for me to learn that they don't have the privilege to value life the way we do.

But despite their poverty and the harshness of their everyday lives most still wear a smile on their faces and they greet you as they pass (usually saying 'Mambo' or 'Habari' meaning 'Hello' or 'How are you'). It makes you wonder if in some ways they have it right.

Eighteen

So it is the day of the charity event and I couldn't quite take in that this was all really happening. I was really doing this. This was huge. I was up and at the train station in Fuengirola to pick Brijan up at 11am. We went straight to the balloon place to sort the balloons for decorating but they asked me to come pick the balloons up at 4pm (no later as they close early on a Saturday and they needed time to get them ready). Not totally convenient for the schedule I had mapped for the day but I would make it work. We headed on from there to El Capricho Resataurante (stopping at the garage as Brijan bought croissants and forced me to eat one before we went in).

I was told the tables would be put in order the night before but it hadn't been done and then I was told I wouldn't have the place all day as I had been promised as they had booked a few people in for lunch. So the tables couldn't be re arranged or set up….. or anything. I was then told I could come get it all ready at 5pm (the event started at 7pm). I was not happy but there wasn't exactly anything I could do about it. Ben arrived with Charlotte then Mike and Paul arrived just after so that the speakers and sound system could be set up for the evening. They did a sound check then we did a run through of the dances (especially the quick dress change in the Dirty Dancing dance).

Piet (Charlotte's neighbor and my friend Lonneke's dad) came down with his video camera and tripod as I had asked if someone could lend me one for the night as I want to record the night. This was something I always wanted to remember and with my parents living in Dubai and the rest of my family in Scotland, I wanted them to see what I had done. So he popped in too to set the camera up.

At about 1pm Brijan and I were the last to leave and headed back to the flat to get showered and ready for the night. By now I was really, really starting to feel the nerves and kept asking myself why the hell I was doing this. What made me think I could pull something this big off and on top of that perform too. I was in all ways out of my comfort zone; the first charity event I have held, a sellout of the restaurant with 60 people attending, having to speak to the whole crowd, performing 3 dances, I mean what was going through my head when I came up with all this? Who did I actually think I was?

Brijan was doing a great job of keeping me as calm and grounded as possible and reassuring me all would work out and be great. But that didn't stop the butterflies in my stomach or my head having 20 things spinning round in it trying to remember everything.

After getting ready it was time to get everything into the car, 3 big hampers of bottles plus all the other raffles prizes, the outfits for the changes in the evening for both of us, a bag of water, plastic cups and some goodies I had got for us doing entertainment to sit in the store room which would act as our dressing room for the night. Then off to Occasions for the balloons where we then had to squeeze them into the back seat of the car. And we were off to the Restaurant once more and it was time for the real deal.

When we arrived they still had the lunch people sitting there chatting over empty glasses and I was furious. Nothing had been sorted at all and there was so much to be done before people started to arrive and I knew people would be coming from 6.30pm. I wasn't going to hang about waiting any longer so I went about sitting and arranging the balloons where I wanted them, Brijan messaged Ben and Charlottle for us asking them to pick us up and McDonalds on their way as we needed to eat still. All they were setting out was paper places with paper napkins (not really ball like). To try and spruce it up a bit I brought some black ribbon and set about wrapping the cutlery in the napkin and tying a bow round them to make it look a tad better. During which the waiters had started to set the tables out properly and had finally got the people to move. Brijan went round the tables putting the center pieces out for me and tying the table numbers to them with the black ribbon (great idea Brijan – looked a lot nicer than just sitting there). After he had cut all the lengths I needed for the napkins.

When Charlotte and Ben arrived with the McDonalds they all tried to usher me outside to eat but I had to finish off my wee jobs first or I would be too distracted (which I ended up being anyway and so nervous I felt sick and could hardly eat a thing and was pacing up and down unable to stay still for 2 minutes).

When all the raffle prizes had been set out on display and all the other wee jobs done, it was into our makeshift dressing room to set all our outfits out for the evening so we were ready and organized for the changes. Then I got myself sorted and out front with my guest list ready for people to arrive.

Nineteen

We started the tour of the hospital by first going to Isaac's office where he greeted me and thanked me for everything I had done and for the amount of money I had raised. He was so grateful especially because I did it without ever having been to Africa, Tanzania or Beta before. He asked me to sign the visitor's book and thanked me once more. Then he asked Alistair and Kristien to tour the hospital with me and told them I could take as many photos as I wanted wherever I wanted. It is so important I have them so people who have donated can see where it is going and hopefully when they see how desperate the hospital is, it will encourage them to donate more; although it is so horrible going round taking photos of people in desperate, dire and heartbreaking situations. But I hope with an account of how it is now people will see the difference we can make for the future and we can see this hospital transform into one that people deserve.

Touring the hospital was like stepping back in time. The equipment they have and the facilities are so old. To be honest I really don't know how to put into words the state of the hospital. I don't think I will ever be able to express the feelings and put across just what it was like touring the hospital. The emotions you go through, the horror of imagining being treated there, the shock of the lack of everything, I guess you can never understand

57

fully until you are standing there in person and seeing it with your own eyes, and even then it is hard to believe.

We started at the beginning, I was shown where the files were kept and if you see the filing system then you wouldn't be surprised that many files get lost (making treatment hard when you don't know their medical history). The filing system is literally lots of sheets of paper crammed into wooden slotted shelves – not ideal. I was shown one of the files, where the man's occupation was peasant, and it turns out this is the case for the majority of the people that come in, they are just known as a peasant. The majority have no record of when they were born so for date of birth it is simply marked as adult. It is so sad to see that people have no record of who they are. The notes are not in a proper order and on top of that such a small amount of information is actually noted down (this has been difficult for the European doctors that are volunteering and they have found it highly frustrating – it is one of the many things they are trying to teach and get the medical staff to do as knowing as much information as possible about symptoms, diagnosis and treatments is highly important).

I was then shown the patients first point of contact which is a little desk set up outside with a weighing scale, blood pressure kit and they note down these things at first contact. The women sitting there doing this exchanged a few words with me and were a little embarrassed but chuffed when I asked if I could take their photo. They were so pleased when I showed them their picture on my camera.

I was then shown the analysis room and consultation rooms. I couldn't believe how old fashioned it all was and the lack of supplies. Then I was totally shocked when I was shown the blood transfusion fridge. On top are bags of blood in blood group order. All they had was four bags of blood for blood group B and that was it. There was quite a stack of bags of blood in the fridge below but that ng free from the government. It is so essential for blood transfusion and it is also required really for all patients. It is such a common thing here, that it is something they should all be screened for.

The room where they test for tuberculosis should be a well ventilated room but here it is like a cupboard with one small window at the top of one wall, which putting the person testing for TB at high risk of catching it themselves. In the lab they are generally using really old machines and old techniques for tests. They have a fancy machine for some tests that had been donated but they have none of the buffers (solutions etc added to generate reactions) needed to get a prognosis, so the machines are sitting there useless, it goes to show how thought needs to go into donations, although it was generous it has been a pointless accessory as there is no money to buy the buffers needed.

I was then shown around the wards. We started with the men's ward. I mean you wouldn't believe the condition. There are a mixed range of old rusty hospital beds that look like they have come from the 1920s. Some have a little foam mattress but not all of them. It is heartbreaking to look at and it just isn't right that people are subjected to these conditions. People deserve so much more. I just can't quite put into words how exactly it looks. But I can tell you it is an unbelievably sad sight and all of us in the first world should really thank our blessings for all we have. Our lives may not be perfect but hell we have things so good.

As you walk between the wards you see old fashioned stretcher trolleys (made me think of something out of the TV series Dads Army) and there are actual visible bloodstains all over the canvas. Doesn't exactly send out a message of hope nor put you in a relaxed state of mind.

We then went to the women's ward which was also being used for children as the children's ward was being used for cholera cases. Again the conditions just aren't up to a moral standard. It was hard to see people in such a desperate state and despite how ill they are or their child or family member they are so desperate to get out as they can't afford to be there. It costs them money to be at the hospital and then it is costing them to not be out trying to make some money. So many are taken home to let them die there, as they think they are too ill anyway, so why spend the money on medicine and hospital fees when they will probably (often in their own opinion) die anyway. In quite a few cases they could survive with some medicine but they look so ill the family doesn't believe it and off they go, where without medicine they are sure to die. We are talking about people of all ages here; babies, kids, adults and the elderly. What a horrible place to be in. So poor you feel it isn't worth spending the tiny amount of money you have to help a member of your family survive or at least die in as much peace as possible. But when you have so little money you are also having to think that using the money on the likes of hospital fees is sacrificing food for other members of the family, like your baby. It really is so hard to take in, I can see the way they are thinking but being privileged enough in life that it is something I have never had to consider, I just can't imagine being in that sort of situation and it is so agonizing to know in so many cases medicine could actually help but they just can't believe it.

While in the women's/children's ward, one child was having seizures. Alistair spotted this and ran over to help. He was angry to find out she had been seizing for a while and the nurse hadn't done a thing. They are just so undereducated. The girl had been diagnosed with cerebral malaria. Kristein ran to get diazepam (this has to be administrated ASAP; after 5 minutes of seizing brain damage can start and it will continue to be more effected the longer they are seizing) which has to be paid for and bought from the pharmacy on the premises (something I plan to change). The diazepam was given after who knows how long the poor child seizing. Only time will tell how bad the long term effects will be. This poor girl who was fighting cerebral malaria a tough enough battle now has a lot more to tackle in life and the future is not looking too bright for her.

It was quite a thing to witness. Then seeing Alistair trying to explain everything and teach the staff there a lesson from what had happened was difficult. It was difficult to see how low the standard of education has been for them to get to where they are and how much damage (not to mention the lives lost) can be down to undereducated staff. It is promising to see volunteers trying to further them but I couldn't help but wonder how much he had said had actually sunk in.

I met one little boy who was finally getting released after being there for malnutrition. He was such a cute little guy but it is painful to think how much he has suffered and how awful it must have been for him but also how likely it was that it could happen again and he could be back here for the same reason, and then your eyes notice the little baby strapped onto his mum's back in a kanga and your heart bleeds at the thought that it could be that poor little ones future too.

I was then shown the labour ward and can I just say it is a terrifying thought that this is where people give birth. I thank my lucky stars that when the day comes that I shall have a baby it will be in a much (no massively) better conditions. To me it is something of nightmares.

In the tiny cupboard like middle waiting room is a mum getting a blood transfusion as she is suffering from post partum hemorrhage. She looks out of it (though it is not due to painkillers – she should be so lucky). She tries to talk to us in Swahili but what she is saying doesn't make sense to anyone there. The scariest part was that the blood wasn't even dripping properly and the nurse hadn't even noticed, it was Kristein that said something then he went to check. It is quite daunting to see the lack of care. He is only there to keep an eye on her, he has nothing else to distract him.

As you leave the labour ward to head to the maternity ward you can see at the back of the main part of the hospital (to the side beyond the men's ward) is a HIV unit where there is recorded to be roughly 530 people with HIV that come to Beta Hospital and we are talking about only the cases that are known. Many more are living with it than is recorded.

As we entered the maternity ward there were plenty of mums and mums to be, most looking so very young. I was introduced to one of the pediatric nurses who had just given birth to a baby boy. This was a lovely moment and to see the pride and happiness in the mother's eyes was beautiful.

Then they showed me the premature room, well they call it a room it is more like a storage cupboard behind the nurses' station (which makes them easily forgotten when they are keeping an eye on and dealing with all the women directly in front of them in the maternity ward). There are four premature babies in at the moment. Three have their mothers there with them but one is alone as his mum is having a blood transfusion (we met her earlier in the labour ward).

When I (and I am sure most of us in the first world) think of a premature ward, we have incubators in mind and lots of machines and tubes etc. Not here. They have some old school oxygen that doesn't have all the settings that they ideally need and for heat they have a few heated mats. However they sometimes need to do a thing called kangaroo therapy (this is when a baby is held naked – except for a hat – to the mothers bare skin so they get her heat and can feel her heartbeat. They are taken from tummy to chest) but the mums don't understand, they think that heated mats must be better and they struggle to get the mums to follow this much needed routine.

The babies were checked and weighed whilst I was there, the lightest weighing just 1.31kg (but he was making great progress as he weighed just 1kg at birth). Another one was sadly losing weight so they were going to have to increase the milk supply but he had been losing weight for a few days now. It is not so promising.

Kristien had asked on my behalf in Swahili if they would be ok for me to take pictures. They didn't object so I took some photos and showed them to the women. They were happy and proud to have their photo taken and we ended up all getting our pictures. Even at such a hard time they had a smile to share.

Kristien and Alistair then showed me a ward that wasn't currently being used that they would love to get turned into a premature ward. They talked to me through how it would be set up and with proper ward with nurses station looking over them, they wouldn't be forgotten. This is a project they both want to try and help with and I think it would be a great use of unused space and increase the chances of the prematures surviving. It was like I was getting pitched an idea. I never thought at 26, people would be pitching an idea to me for me to help them build a ward at a hospital.

As we moved towards the surgical theatre they pointed out a building set right back where mothers due to give birth but will definitely need a c-section or are having difficulties can stay cheaply so they are close when the time comes. Though most still can't afford this.

The surgical theatres are like something out of a horror film. It is like something out of the dark ages and it felt so eerie inside. It certainly didn't look like the most sanitary and hygienic place. It looks rusty and old and really quite scary. I have to say I was glad to get out.

As we walked out we saw an x-ray propped into the ground by a metal pole in the sun. This is how they dry them. Most unusual thing to see but also admittedly quite smart.

We walked down to the storage room where the medical supplies go and outside piled high were all the medicines and supplies that I had purchased with the money raised through so many people's generous donations.

I couldn't quite believe how much was there. Isaac and a few other members of staff came to help unpack everything so there could be a stock check and everything logged before put away in the storage room.

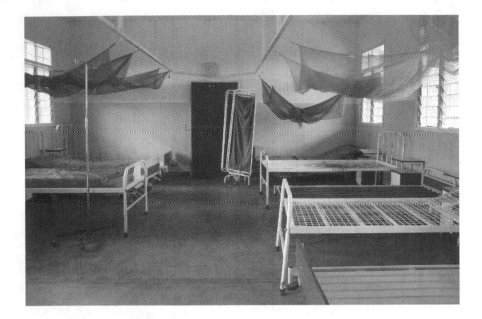

What the wards look like

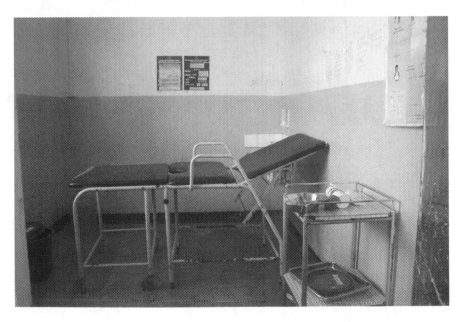

Labour Ward

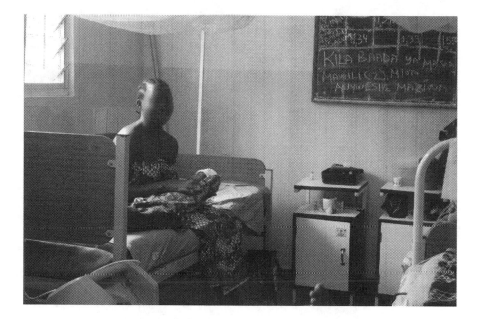

Mother with Premature Baby

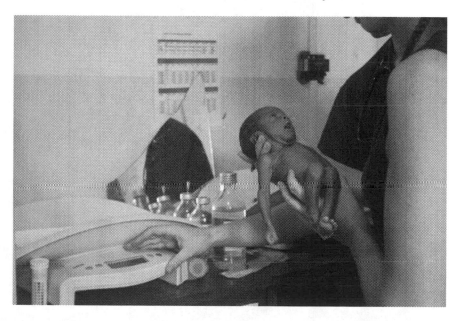

Premature baby

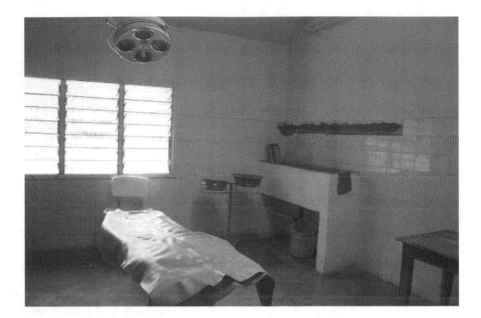

The Surgical Theatre

Medical Supplies from the Money Raised

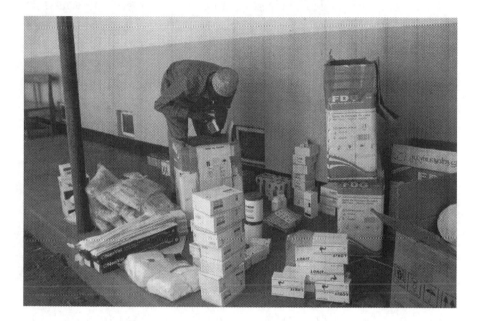

Medical Supplies from the Money Raised

Me with all the Medical Supplies bought
with the Money Raised

As we were unpacking Kristien and Alistair said it was like Christmas and the others just kept thanking me. Kristien was amazing at letting me know what some of the things were and how they would help. It was nice knowing how they would be used and how they are beneficial. When all was unpacked and they were logging, Alistair suggested I should see the room before it was all stocked up. I was shown the storage room before anything could be put away and to see the sorry state of it was incredible, I was gob smacked at how bare the shelves were. I knew they were in desperate need but I really had no idea how bad it was. I could count on my hands how much was actually on the shelves. Seeing how bad it actually was I now understood why Isaac kept saying it came at the right time. There was medicine that would be effective immediately (for example for the cholera).

When I went back outside one of the guys shook my hand and thanked me and told me he was "100% happy". I felt so touched.

When we got back to the house Lisa still wasn't well and she desperately wanted to go. She felt we should go to the town of Morogoro and stay the night there then get on our way back first thing tomorrow morning. Personally I felt it made more sense staying the night in the house where we have doctors and if she still felt she needed to get home we could leave first thing in the morning. Morogoro is just an hour and a half from Beta, so I didn't really see what it was achieving, but she really wasn't well and we don't know what she had. I can understand her wanting her own room where she didn't have to share a toilet.

So with her mind made up I got myself packed up. We waited for Isaac who wanted to say bye before we left. As we waited I sat with the little boy who liked to come and hang outside the house. Kristien translated for me as we tried to speak a little. He really was such a cutie. He watched us unloading the car of the jumpers and some bags of toys. I felt so bad unloading all these things in front of him as he sat there with nothing. The clothes on his back were old, dirty and ripped but these were for the orphanage and

I had no right to give them away. However I had brought a few football tops with me, so I picked them up and let him choose which one he wanted. He was so happy and kept looking at me before he would touch any of the tops.

Kristien let him know that I said he could have whichever top he wanted. He smiled at me and asked if he could have the blue one as blue was his favourite colour. I handed him the blue top and he held it to his chest like it was the most amazing thing I could have given him.

Kristien went back inside and I sat on the ground by the front door with him. He just sat there holding onto his top and smiling and looking at me. Now and again he would touch my skin or stroke my hair (this is what a lot of them do as they are so taken by the white skin and blonde hair). He didn't say anything, he just wanted to have some company, someone to sit with. It made me well up inside but I couldn't show him my emotions as he wouldn't understand why I was feeling that way. You need to stay strong.

I look at him and I don't just see the obvious; he has no shoes, the t-shirt has big rips and holes as does the shorts he is wearing, that not just his clothes but he is dirty and not exactly looking very healthy. I see more than that. I see a child that has already gone through more than we would ever like to acknowledge a child can go through. I can see that there is fear, uncertainty and pain. But also I saw strength and hope. The little boy stole a place in my heart as I sat there with him. I wanted so much to just take him with me. To help him but obviously I can't.

I popped back inside and I was chatting to Kristien who told me what she knew about him. That he came round there a lot but just sat outside. That he was an orphan but there was no space left in the orphanage for them to take him. That as far as they knew the locals in the village did what they could to help him out (as with a few kids in the same position) but with them all being poor and struggling there isn't much they can do. She doesn't know what happened to his family. He is guessed to be about 7 years old. Hearing all this just broke my heart more. I mean how awful and scary must that be. To be left roaming on your own at 7 years old. Nobody to protect you, love you, guide you or feed you. I wouldn't know how to cope at my age never mind his.

We then heard him at the door calling my name. he would never come in, but he cracked the door open slightly and called my name. we went to the door and Kristien told me he was asking for a plastic bag. She went and got one for him as I sat next to him outside. When he got it he gently folded it up and placed it in the bag and held it to his chest, like it was the most treasured gift he has ever been given. To not cry at that moment was so hard, but I had to remember what he has been through has been so much worse and I had to be strong for him. I got my camera and took a photo of him and then showed it to him. He was so happy and asked for one of us both. He smiled so much when I showed him the photo and that warmed my heart. When you see a smile like that, you cant help but smile yourself. It pains me to think of him alone and him just kicking around all day. He deserves to be loved and looked after, he deserves an education and chance in life, he deserves food and shelter. He doesn't deserve to be where he is. It is not his fault, he was born into the wrong part of the world. It is all just so wrong. If I could have I would have wrapped my arms around him and taken him home.

The Young Lad who will forever live in my heart

I then go in and sit and chat to Kristien and Alistair about everything we saw at the hospital and we discussed what the hospital really needs, what is a priority and what direction I will go in as far as supporting the hospital goes.

Isaac arrives and I tell him firmly I have had chats with the doctors and from what I have seen, heard and been told; I expect to see an emergency box placed on every ward with things like diazepam (only used in emergencies and time is of the essence). That the doctors will tell him what really needs to be in the emergency boxes and I want it taken from my donations and placed there. I also said that I will continue to support Beta but my next lot of money raised will be to help get someone trained at a higher level. Clearly the level of education is of too low a standard so if bit by bit we can raise their education and medical standard they will become more self sufficient.

Isaac seemed happy with this plan and he thanked me once again.

We then went out to the car to head to Morogoro. It was actually quite sad saying bye to Kristien, Alistair and Emma. It felt a little hard driving off and waving bye to them all standing with Isaac on the porch waving goodbye. It is weird how you can feel so attached to people, a place and a cause in such a small space of time. I felt like I had been there for so much longer than I had and I felt it was far too early to go.

However I also feel so much more determined and motivated to do all I can to help the Beta Hospital than ever. I am now lying in a hotel room in Morogoro (that Lisa paid for as it wasn't exactly part of our itinerary) thinking about my next plan of action. How I will raise money, how I will get it here, how to arrange a long term plan, how I will ensure the terms and conditions are met. There is so much to do and I am so desperate to crack on.

I am also lying on this hotel room bed feeling guilty that I have so much when so many have so little. We can escape so easily from what is going on, Lisa feels ill so we can jump in a car and go. But they can't do that. This is everyday life for them. Why should I have a bed to lie on, why should I have bottled water by my side. It is just so hard to walk away and not feel guilty for the privileges I have.

Twenty

Kristien is from Belgium and has been up at Beta Hospital now for 10 months voluntarily. In a few weeks she will finally go home but her emotions are mixed about leaving. I can totally understand that. But when you do eventually have to move on to a paid job to survive, no matter how difficult it is to do.

Kristien has done a lot in Beta and the people have become a big part of her life and heart. She even leant some money to one of the nurses so she could finish a part of her education, knowing there was a high chance she would never see the money again – though she did.

Alistair and Emma are married and have been at Beta for just a few weeks but will be there for a total of 3 months. They may not have been there long but they have plenty of stories already.

Kristien and Alistair have told me many stories about the hospital and also we had a frank discussion about charity work. Through my discussions with them I have come to realize how important it it to have an end goal. As great as it is donating you need to think about what you donate, how it will help, long term help and how to help them be eventually self-sufficient and no longer NEED you. I guess I hadn't really thought it all through like that before.

It made me change tact with how I would proceed with fundraising and how to use the money so that it would help them in the long term and help them to start helping themselves more.

Through a lot of their stories and what I witnessed it became apparent what they really need is properly trained staff.

An example of how staff was effecting the hospital was how one of the premature babies died and how it was totally preventable. A poor woman had gone through 3 unsuccessful pregnancies (miscarriages and still births) and she finally delivered but far too prematurely. The reason this baby did not survive was because the nurses did not feed the baby. The baby needs to be woken and fed every hour but this poor baby was neglected by the nurses.

The mothers (and to be honest the majority of nurses) don't understand the needs of a premature baby. They are educated that if a baby needs anything it will cry, so because the babies are not crying they believe the baby is fine. However premature babies do not realize they are hungry, they aren't developed enough for that yet, so they will not cry for food. They struggle to get that through to them, especially the mums.

When the nurse did not attend the baby the mum did and said nothing as she thought her baby was content and that was why it did not cry.

The nurses were busy in the maternity ward (where a woman also bled out that night) and with the premature babies and their mothers being hidden in 'storage cupboard' they were forgotten and neglected.

Over here there is no punishment for such a thing. You don't have to worry about negligence charges, though Kristien and Alistair try to explain to the nurses that something like that would mean prison in most other places.

It is such a heartbreaking story and you can see the pained and frustrated looks on their faces as they recount the story from what was going on my first night in Beta.

The woman that bled out my first night was the emergency that Alistair had ran into the house to collect his things for. The woman had internal bleeding and the nurses were told to administer some medication. She was then left and nobody checked up on her, yes that is correct they did not check up on a woman suffering from internal bleeding. Then when Alistair and Kristien went to do their nightly rounds before bed they found her in a mess and tried to save her life, sadly to no avail.

Then to make matters worse when they checked her notes the medics had told the nurses to give her a drug that has a side effect of causing the blood to flow faster. So all it did was make her bleed out. The poor, poor woman.

They went over all these things with everyone. When they asked what had happened they were told she suddenly bled out. You don't just all of a sudden bleed out. I have no medical training and I know that. This is what they were trying to deal with. Then the next night it nearly happened again, but thankfully this time they caught it and the woman made it through.

So all this has really highlighted that a major problem is the lack of educational standard that needs to be dealt with pronto. This is why I have decided to go in that direction with my planning and why it is so essential. Medicine is great but without people who really know what they are doing, it isn't so useful.

I will still raise for medicine too as it is also essential. But the first amount raised will go on sending someone for extra training.

I have utmost respect for Kristien and Alistair for doing what they are. Hands on making a difference and saving peoples lives. I also really hope their project for a premature ward can get up and running.

Twenty One

6th December 2015 17:45

I am hoping that whatever it is that Lisa has I do not end up getting. I really am glad that I had my own room last night. I don't want to sound bad and I do feel awful saying it but I don't want to get ill. It would really suck getting ill in a country I don't know, where I am here alone and we don't even know what it is Lisa caught. I know that being in a car for so many hours together put me at high risk depending what it is that is actually wrong with her. Here is hoping I stay healthy.

So I got up at around 6ish again this morning, got my bucket shower and my things sorted to travel back to Dar. I still have a feeling that I am leaving without doing enough at the hospital but I have to keep in mind that the most important things were done. So I sat and waited for Lisa to say she was up and ready for our drive back.

We travelled straight back with no stops until we got to my hotel at Bahari Beach. The drivers on the road were particularly bad and really dangerous. It is crazy how a lot of these guys drive.

Once back at the hotel I thought I should make the most of the fact that I was by the beach and with a couple hours left of the sun, I quickly changed and headed down for a stroll along the beach.

It was so peaceful and relaxing. It gave me a chance to take in all my thoughts and deal with all the emotions of the last few days.

I then went back to my room where I was messaging Brijan, we are hoping to catch one another on skype at some point. I hope so. It would be good to chat about everything and maybe next time he will make it here with me. I think it would be a great experience and with me having been here already I would know what we were doing and where to go etc.

The sea here is so clear and the sand is white. The people are so friendly too. I feel so relaxed and at peace in this hotel. A weird sensation after all the emotions of Beta. I can understand how this place can get under peoples skin and how they can never totally let it go.

Now I am showered (which was an amazing feeling) and sitting on some rocks on the beach as the sun sets. I am so grateful for all my blessings.

Twenty Two

As the first people started to arrive I thought I really was going to be sick. All that kept going through my head was "shit this is really real and I have to make sure everyone has a good time and what made me think I could do all this".

But I was soon distracted greeting people, checking their tickets and ticking them off the guest list. Everyone was being so supportive as they arrived and it was nice to know that so many people had my back.

As everyone was seated and the night was about to begin I got my first rush of terror. Mike my amazing compare went up to greet everyone (and he was wonderfully funny at all the right times throughout the night) and then he introduced me to the stage (adding a little funny skit that I only found out about 2 minutes beforehand and I wasn't entirely sure what I was to do – but it worked fantastically). I then had to do the serious part of the evening doing a wee speech about why we were all there. I had planned on writing it before the night but decided to just get up and speak from my heart. Following now is the speech (which I have written from the video taken from the night as to be honest I was so nervous I wouldn't have been able to tell you what I had said otherwise):

"This night is not about me, The Jersey Boys or anyone else; it is about raising money for an amazing cause. Over in Beta they have together created a Hospital, orphanage and school for children. They have already done that and that has been set up but that is not enough. They need medicine, they need stethoscopes, they need teachers, they need school supplies and I am going over there to volunteer, whilst I am over there I will be staying in a little hut with no electricity, no running water but again this is not about me. These people live like this ever day, and in this world we forget the difference between wanting something and needing something. We don't NEED half the thongs we have and these people ask for nothing and they have nothing. Tonight I want you to have fun, I want you to enjoy yourself but please bear that in mind, when you are buying your raffle tickets and everything but bear that thought in mind. It is coming up to Christmas, how much you are going to spend on Christmas presents that half the things people are going to complain or return or they don't want. These kids, they are not asking for Christmas presents, I just want to give them the medicines they deserve. If you ave been following me on facebook I have been complaining about the amount of vaccinations I have had to have – eight – I am terrified of needles, it is the most terrifying thing for me and the worst part of this whole event BUT I have the PRIVILIDGE to get vaccinated against these diseases these kids don't, they are children. The difference between the life I have been given and the life they've got is that I was born in the right country. So please tonight please, please dig deep and bear the kids in mind and lets give them the chance they deserve."

I spoke a few words before and after but that was my speech. Not the best one in the world but it got the message out and it came from my heart and I said what I truly believe. Though I ended up not having to stay in a hut, I didn't get to do all the volunteer work I had wanted and hoped to do but it all rang true and I gave them all the information I had at the time.

Once that was over I actually felt a bit better and could breathe a little until I realized as Paul and Ben started their Kings of Swing set, that when they finished I would be up there doing the dirty dancing set. I checked all was good with Brijan and that Mike was ok and knew what he was doing. I checked the waiting staff were fine then got a hug from Brijan outside before I went to get myself changed for the big dance.

I glanced through the window at everyone before I went into the makeshift dressing room with Charlotte and all looked good. People were eating and everyone looked happy and the boys were on top form as always, I knew that was the one thing I needn't worry about. The boys would give an excellence performance, and really as long as I have that the night would be ok. That put me at ease a little bit before Charlotte ushered me in to help me change.

Twenty Three

7th December 2015 19:39

I am sitting on the balcony of my hotel room. The weather is beautiful. Not too hot with a lovely breeze. The sound of the waves mixed with the breeze rustling the leaves is so peaceful and I feel so relaxed. I am loving this.

I was up at 6.30am. Got up, ready and down to breakfast. There was more going on this morning compared to the last time. I knew better now than to go to the pool too early, so after grabbing my bag for the beach and changing into my sarong, I headed for the beach instead.

I placed my things down on the sun bed and went for a stroll along the beach. It was dead nearly all the way along and I enjoyed having it all to myself.

When I got back to the sun bed and had got myself settled the security guy came over and started to chat to me. He told me his name is Jimmy (not very African) and welcomed me to Tanzania. I thanked him, introduced myself and settled back down as Jimmy moved on. He was back two minutes later and started chatting away to me again. Bless. He stood there talking for 20 minutes.

He said he was sad I was married (I am wearing a ring and claiming to be married while I am here, as I was advised this would be the best thing to do over here) as he would like a white wife because African women had small brains and all they want to do is talk. I tried to tell him non-African men are the same, to which he told me he didn't believe me. He told me on the TV the white women are always busy and work very hard. I wasn't going to go into trying to explain media and programmed representation. Don't get me wrong, many women (and men) do work very hard and are very busy but we have so many that are the opposite. It is a very drastic over generalization.

Anyway after chatting to me for at least 20 minutes he says one of the days I am here he would take me out the hotel and show me the town and the people. I smiled and said thanks. I also then said it was time for a swim in the sea before he could take it any further. It was a very kind thing to offer but I will stay on the safe side. if I wasn't alone then no doubt I would wonder into town and explore but I am solo and security has to come first, though I would love to see and experience more.

So I went for a little dunk in the sea. It was so warm and the water so clear, it was so beautiful and wonderful. When I got back to my sun bed I got my book out straight away. It was nice chatting to Jimmy but it was time to relax and switch off for a bit. I brought the book 'mini-shopaholic' by Sophie Kinsella. Something nice and lighthearted but the irony did hit me.

I had a lovely day on the beach. You really cant beat that view and for the first time in a long time I do feel relaxed. Though my mind cant totally switch off and I cant help but feel guilty that I have been lying there chilled out when I am in a country surrounded by people with so little. That is a hard feeling to budge.

I managed a skype chat with my mum which was nice. It was good to chat to someone about everything that has happened and all the emotions that I have been going through. It really is a rollercoaster. I haven't been able to catch Brijan which is a shame. I do miss him and would love to tell him about everything. I was able to chat a bit on whatsapp with my sis Charlotte though and that was really nice. It was great to hear from her.

I chilled in the room for a wee while, did my laundry in the sink (it was really dusty and dirty up in Beta) and then got myself showered and changed. I decided to go for another stroll along the beach, one of my favourite things to do. The sun was starting to sink in the sky, it is the perfect time for a walk along the beachfront.

By now the beach is pretty busy down past the hotel's section. It is the weekend after all. As I walked along the beach it became apparent I was the only white person, so as you can imagine I got a bit of attention but never in an uncomfortable or bad way.

A few times a wee group of kids came running up to me with big smiles and said hi with a little wave, before running of giggling when I waved and said hi back. It was super cute. A few guys also said hi as I walked past and again on my way back. Nobody was disrespectful or rude. They are such a lovely, polite people here.

Then as I was getting closer to the hotel again, I saw a wedding party. They were on the beach having their photos taken. It was so lovely to see. I went and sat on a rock close by and watched the sky as it started to change colour. It was all just so picturesque.

One guy from the wedding came over to me and told me he loved to dance. There had been a band playing by the pool since late afternoon and he began dancing to the music in front of me. It was so surreal. I lightly clapped when he was finished and he shook my hand and introduced himself as James. He asked me my name and then if I spoke Swahili. When I told him no and he asked why not and told me he wanted me to know Swahili.

He obviously wasn't as practiced in English but he said he wants to make it better. Then some of the others from the wedding party came over too and one guy who had his phone in his hand asking for a photo with me. I agreed and then next thing they were all wanting a photo with me. So I had my photo taken with a few men and women and then two adorable little children. I don't know why they all wanted their photo with me but they were so happy about it.

They thanked me so many times and headed towards the restaurant of the hotel. James however stayed and spoke to me a little more. He told me he was an engineer for motorbikes and how he hopes to have his own business. He asked me my thoughts of Tanzania and was very happy when I said it was very beautiful.

I then thanked him for talking to me and shook his hand saying it was a pleasure to meet him, making my excuses to go. It was such a strange but really nice occurance. I just cant get over how hospitable and friendly they are here.

That brings me back to sitting here peacefully on my balcony.

Twenty Four

I stepped out the "dressing room" with Charlotte and Brijan (who had come in to change too). We stood outside and took in the fresh air. All my calmness had totally gone out the window and now I was thinking how nervous I was and how much I didn't want to mess up. We had worked so hard and it had got good and I really didn't want to blank.

Char took a quick photo of Brijan and I, we shared a quick hug and Brijan told me it would all be great. Then before I knew it I heard Mike on the microphone introducing us. My heart was pounding so hard I thought it was about to pop through my chest, my mouth was so dry, my legs felt like jelly and my whole body was shaking (I was trying to will my body to get its act together).

I walked onto the floor and the music started. Brijan walked down to me and to be honest the rest of it is a bit of a blur. It went really well and we nailed the lift (though we never got to the point we could do it without my hands on his shoulders) but it didn't run totally smooth and there was a little problem with me getting the dress back on as Charlotte couldn't get it done back up but I just pulled the top part down and carried on. It went down really well and I did enjoy myself. It was worth all the work and nerves that came with it.

Following our dance it was a quick change for Brijan then out to do the Jersey Boys tribute with Ben and Paul. They were totally on point as always. Charlotte and myself joined them for a couple of the songs as the Jersey Girls dancing behind them, just like we do in Legends Cabaret Bar. But they caught me by surprise when they got me up on a chair and Brijan danced for me (and on me) to the song Stay (also from Dirty Dancing). I was a little shocked and embarrassed but I absolutely loved it haha.

As the boys came off Charlotte and I did our dance routines; "All that jazz" was first and then a very quick change for our 60s medley. It went so well and I was really proud of us, but even more so Charlotte because I know how much out of her comfort zone she was and how nervous she was too. I really appreciate her putting herself out there to do all that for my Charity night.

The Blues Brothers Tribute followed us (Brijan and Ben). They were amazing of course. They have great energy in their routines and it is such a fabulous show. Charlotte and I were trying to get the last of the raffle tickets sold and then counted and ready before the boys finished as the raffle would be drawn at the end of their act.

Twenty Five

8th December 2015 22.40

Lying on the bed at The Mayfair Hotel and I have no idea how I am going to get to sleep. I am so excited for the safari starting tomorrow, though I won't actually be doing anything tomorrow. It is a long drive to get to the National Park so by the time we get up there it will be too late to go round and see the animals. But it is still the beginning of the journey and something I have wanted to do for such a long time, especially growing up with all my parents stories about the safaris they went on. I know I really need to get to sleep as I am getting picked up at 6.30am, so I will need to check out at 6am, meaning I will need to be up at 5am. I should really be sound asleep already but I really don't know how I will manage it.

This morning I was up at my usual 6.30am, went down for my breakfast and back to the room to make sure I was pretty organized for check out, which wasn't till 12pm so I went down to the beach with my book to chill for a little while.

Mum caught me on skype so we had a little chat about her trip to Scotland, me being there a few days with her, my safari (so excited if you didn't know) and Christmas etc. As soon as I was off the phone the wee security man started to talk to me (not Jimmy, this was another one), I had seen him hovering as I was talking to mum. So I chatted a little (about football – they really love football here) then I got on with my reading.

At 10.30am I headed back to the room to get showered and pack up the last bits and bobs. Then a sad moment as I closed the door. I have thoroughly enjoyed my there. I felt so comfortable at this hotel.

So I got checked out and they got a wee driver for me who chatted a bit (but not as much as the others so far) as we made our way to the Mayfair Hotel. It is more the middle of town. I got checked-in and was shown to my room. The rooms are ok but nothing like I was just in. I am not complaining at all as I am still above and beyond privileged compared to most. I looked out the window and it is a stark reminder of how lucky I am. I see 5 kids playing on an unbuilt second floor of a house. No walls, no safety, no shoes, no toys. Just playing on what was essentially a flat rooftop, just 5 kids between the ages of about 3 and 7 alone, creating their own fun. It hits me once again how lucky and privileged I am. They all had the biggest smiles on their faces though.

I have a room that is clean enough and has a comfy bed. It is crazy how much we take for granted. I really hope I don't ever forget this feeling. The feeling of just how lucky I am with everything I have in my life. I think we could learn a lot from people here. They know how to be happy with what they have. Don't get me wrong we should have goals and strive to do and be our best but along the way we should be happy with the life we are leading every day and be thankful for what we have.

I went out for a little walk as I had no water. According to the website there is a little supermarket but that isn't the case. So I wandered round the little outdoor plaza next to the hotel and went back to my room. The hotel is in a more run down area so I did not want to wander alone for too long.

My hotel room phone rang just after I got back and I had assumed it was a repeat of the first hotel with someone getting the wrong room but actually it was the receptionist saying Mike Philips (my parents friend and my brothers godfather) was on the line, would I like his call to be put through. Of course I asked for the call to be put through and I spoke to Mike and arranged to meet him at the Yacht club this evening at 5.45pm. He had a meeting there at 5pm so the plan was for me to arrive at the back end of it.

So I set about organizing my bags for the safari and getting showered to go out. Now I had tried to be ahead of the game and be organized so I had done my washing by hand in the sink and hung it out to dry. Only problem being I now needed something to wear but everything was now damp, which meant putting on damp clothing to go to the yacht club (though it soon dried).

I got a taxi downstairs and he dropped me off at the yacht club. For some reason (seems ridiculous to me) taxis are not allowed to drive into the yacht club so security made me get out at the gate and walk in (it is only a few seconds walk so it didn't bother me, but I do find it a weird set up when they have a drive up to the entrance).

So in I go, looking round for Mike, only problem is I don't know what he looks like (this being the first time I would meet him – the call he made to me earlier being the first I had spoken to him) making it kind of difficult. I had hoped he would have spotted me when I walked in, so I gave him a call and seeing as he had been sitting round a corner it was no wonder he hadn't seen me.

He said he just had to finish up his meeting so I said I would wait at the bar. As I was getting seated, Mike noticed a man one seat down was a guy he knows well called Steve. So he introduced us and told him to buy me a drink and look after me until he got back. I was mortified but Steve was very polite and chatty and bought me a coca-cola. For someone else to tell someone to buy me a drink is not something I am accustomed to and I find it really embarrassing.

Anyway, Steve was an easy person to chat to, he told me about his sons and grandchildren and asked me questions about my life. We were chatting away when Mike joined us. He told Steve to shut up, that I was his guest and that the chat shouldn't revolve around him. I guess this is their banter but I felt a bit awkward and bad for poor Steve who had been so nice.

Well the three of us chatted for a bit, then one of Steve's sons came to pick him up. Steve said bye and told me he had a handsome son in Capetown who still wasn't married – that I should make Capetown my next visit haha.

So Mike and I sat and chatted. I filled him in a bit on what the family are doing now and he told me some stories of the time my parents lived in Dar and then at some point we ended up on some political topics. Then I got dropped off by the hotel by Mike. He dropped me on the road near the gate and he sat and made sure I got in ok. There were two groups of young lads outside (naturally I felt a bit wary – no matter where you are) and the security guy took his time coming to the gate and unpaddlocking it and taking off the chains but I had no hassle.

Straight in, up to bed and here I am sitting wondering how on earth I will manage to sleep. Really need to though as it is an early start and a long drive.

Twenty Six

The raffle was going great and then there was a little twist and it went from great to AMAZING! The wonderful Geraldine and Gary Haynes won the dinner for two at Sai Indian Restaurant in La Cala however they were flying the next day so they brought the voucher back up and said we could auction it off. We were thinking we would get 20 euros or so as it was a 40 Euro voucher, but things took off. My boss Andrea Gallacher (who had had a wine or two – bottles I think not glasses haha) got into a bidding war with Charlie Mullins. It was so funny as they kept going at each other from opposite sides of the room until finally Charlie outbid her with 500Euros being paid for the voucher (which Charlie being the sweetheart that he is handed to me and said to go out with my "sister" for dinner after all our hard work. I couldn't of course walk in and use a voucher donated to my charity night so I told my sis to go out and have dinner with Ben).

The boys ended what was a fabulous night with a mixture of upbeat and dance music. Everyone had a fabulous time and we raised a fantastic amount of 2,100 Euros. I was so touched and stunned to have raised so much. It had been my goal to raise 1,500 Euros altogether, so to have raised that in one evening was just out of this world.

Brijan, Charlotte, Mike, Ben and Paul put so much effort into making the night fun, entertaining, smooth and brilliant and

I really don't know how I could have pulled it off without such amazing friends and support around me. I count my blessings for having these people in my life.

When I was hearing thanks from everyone and how much they enjoyed the evening it meant so much to me. So many people said to me that it was the best night they had been to and they hoped this wouldn't be the only one I organized. So when I announced the amount we had raised I also announced that the Beta Ball would now become an annual event.

When all was done and people were starting to get ready to go, Charlotte's Mum and Dad took me to one side and told me how proud they were of me and how I should be proud of myself for what I had achieved. It meant so much to me and it was so unexpected I had to excuse myself a moment and have a little cry. It was such a lovely thing to hear and also the relief I had pulled it all off just came over me for a minute. Charlotte came and found me as did her mum Jenny and gave me a hug. Then Brijan came to get me and he told me he was proud too and how proud I should be of everything I had done. He gave me a kiss and we went to get ourselves ready to go home.

Twenty Seven

9th December 2015 21:09

I am so shattered after today and lying here incredibly full so I am quite sleepy but I will quickly fill in todays adventures. So I got up at 5am after a restless sleep. Got ready, checked out and only had to wait a few minutes before the guy arrived in the safari car. So his name is Salim, he has two children (one boy of 2 years and a girl of 7 years old). He has lived in many places throughout Tanzania. We chatted about this as we made our way out of Dar in the awful traffic. We picked the cook up on our way. I didn't catch his name but he has two daughters (10 and 12 years old). He is originally from Dodoma but lives in Dar. He is divorced but tries to visit his girls regularly.

It was after picking up the cook that I learnt that nobody else would be on the safari with us. I had thought there would be others joining us, but it turned out I would be on a private safari.

So we had a long drive but it was interesting to see how the scenery keeps changing. At one point we drove through Mikumi National Park as the main road cuts right through it, this is maybe 4 or 5 hours into our drive. I'm not quite sure though. Anyway driving through there we saw some elephant, water hog, baboons, impala, vultures and zebra in the close distance and we had to stop as some zebra crossed the road. I mean it was literally a zebra crossing! What an amazing sight it was to see.

We stopped for lunch. I had a chicken burger, a proper chicken breast – it was very filling, especially after eating so little over the past week. I was very full. We then drove into the town of Iringa where our chef popped to the market (a street market that is) and bought some supplies.

As we drove from the market onto Hill Top Lodge the driver handed me a banana to keep me going till dinner. I was still feeling really full from lunch so I just left it on my lap. After a few minutes the cook looked over and saw I hadn't touched the banana and he told me in a stern and powerful tone I was to eat my banana. I was taken aback and did as I was told (Brijan would like this guy, he is always having a go at me about eating).

As we drove the guys told me a story about a group they had taken on safari earlier in the year. There was a Scottish guy and on their last night he shared a bottle of whisky with the whole group and they all got really drunk. They were camping out and he got so drunk he went for a pee and managed to get himself lost, unable to find his way back to his tent. They found him walking back into the camp at 6am and they asked if he slept well, he said no he had been wondering round trying to find the camp all night. By the tracks they found out he had literally been walking round the camp in a circle all night. Too funny. But he was also incredibly lucky, because the reality is there are wild animals walking around and he could have got himself in serious trouble. But it was a funny story.

We then headed to the lodge where we were to stay. It was 7pm by the time we arrived here and it was dark. We were on a beaten track and sometimes it was a little scary as you cant see that far ahead and I was aware of the fact as we were going up and up; there must be a rather large drop to one side. We drove past a lorry that had half fallen off the road and dangling over the cliff edge. It made my hands sweat just seeing that (it was the back end that was hanging off and everyone was out and safe).

We thankfully made it safely to Hill Top Lodge. As we drove up the wee track to the lodge some wild dogs ran past us and you could hear the wild animals in the vicinity. Only I was to stay up here, Salim and the cook go back down and camp out. I was the only guest in the whole place. I was taken to my lodge (yes an individual lodge not just a room). The place is set up with a reception and eating area at the front (open air with a thatched roof) and then spread out were lots of individual lodges. Each one is named after an animal and they are set quite far apart. You have to climb a stony uneven path to get to each lodge. I was thankful that mine wasn't too high or too far away but it was hard to see as it was already dark as we walked up and I hadn't got my torch out but I was thinking how glad I was that I had brought my torch in my bag for getting back down for dinner.

The lodge is cute and there was actually a solar lantern inside so I can use that to go back down. A good idea to have, though would have been useful for getting up here. So I got my things sorted and headed (carefully) back down for dinner. I wasn't feeling too hungry but they had made an effort just for me so I felt obliged to eat a bit. As I am the only one staying here there was one place set up. The dining are consists of 3 tables of 6 and on one of them was a lantern, a glass, placemat and cutlery all set up just for me. At first I thought it looked a bit sad and lonely but then when I sat down I actually felt like a special guest.

To my shock they had made a 3 course meal. Soup to start (delicious by the way – though I daren't ask what it was) but a big portion with bread (I had originally assumed this was dinner and would alone usually be a meal for me) then four big bowls came out; one with rice, one with some kind of meat (I don't know what it was but for some reason I have a feeling I ate Pumba), one with potatoes and one with green beans and carrots. All that went through my head was 'how on earth would I manage this?' and

I felt like I had to eat everything. Over here with so many people going without food you feel despicable if you leave anything uneaten. It is like a slap in everyone's face. I was already so full though and I tried to eat as much as I could but being so stuffed I was struggling. It was very nice and my mum would be so proud at all these things I was eating and I didn't even know what I was eating most of the time (I have always been an incredibly fussy eater). When I told them I had enough to eat they kept asking if I was sure. I explained it was wonderful but I just could not eat that amount at which point my plates were cleared and a crepe came out for my dessert. I thanked them so much for dinner and apologized for not eating it all but I was just too full. I made my way back to my lodge (Cheetah Lodge).

It was quite a freaky walk back. All alone with only a solar lantern to see with, knowing there are wild animals around and trying to walk up a stony hill. It was done at a quick pace and trying to get the key in the lock to get in the lodge was done with a little tremble.

Now I am half asleep feeling a bit sick due to being so full and hoping I will get a good night's sleep.

Twenty Eight

A few days after the ball and I was still reeling off the buzz from the ball but there was still plenty of exciting things happening in my life before I set off on my journey to Tanzania. My brother, sister-in-law (ok technically they aren't married but she is still family in my eyes) and my little 6 month old niece arrived for a 4 day holiday. It was great to get some time with them (especially finally getting some time with my niece). While they were here though I had to set a few hours aside and did a TV interview in Marbella about my charity and how we had one more event to go.

But before that I had a great four days with the family, then the day after they left I was driving back up to Torremolinos to get Brijan and his stuff as he moved in with me. I was quite nervous, after living on my own for so many years and being used to my own space and routine the idea of someone else being there and how it would go scared me slightly, but on the other hand I know we get on so well and we always have such a laugh and good time together I knew deep down I had nothing to worry about.

As I would be away for most of the "Christmas period" we decided to put up our Christmas decorations early. So we had a fab night a week after Brijan moving in where we decorated our tree, put up our decorations, listening to Christmas music, Brijan cooked dinner and we had a wee glass of Rose (or two). It was perfection really.

Then it was time for the last event. My friend Laura Oldfield had organized an event at Jacksons Bar in Fuengirola for Kids under her business Kids Parties Spain. Brijan and I went down to help out with the tombola and raffle (I was dressed up as Cinderella and Brijan kindly took plenty of photos for us). There was a magician, party music, games, balloon man, face painting and plenty entertainment. With some other Disney princesses, Olaf and Spiderman also making appearances. It was another great success and what a fabulous event Laura had orchestrated. I am so lucky to have such amazing and supportive friends.

Twenty Nine

10th December 2015 21:16

I woke this morning to a beautiful sunrise. The sky was the most stunning view. I was up at 6am. I didn't have the best night's sleep. I woke up because I felt something fluttering by my ear and it kept coming back. Totally didn't like that and it is literally pitch black, you really can't see a thing. With no lights anywhere you can put your hand right in front of you with your palm touching your nose and not see it. So I found my way to the parting of the mosquito net and got my hands through and found the lantern and had a look around the bed. The mosquito net obviously trapped something in with me or there is a hole somewhere is what I was thinking. At first I didn't see what it was then I saw this massive moth (to my relief - you should see the bugs out here). I managed to get it out as quick as possible in order to avoid letting anything in. Then it took me a while to get back to sleep. Then the little cat that watched me eating dinner (think I forgot to mention that) must have found me and sat by the door meowing for ages. That was another disturbance but then I must have drifted off to sleep.

So I got up at 6am, a wee shower and sorted myself out. Got all my stuff packed and ready to go. I headed down for my breakfast at the time we agreed over dinner the night before – 7am. I just kept thinking to myself - please don't be too much. I was still feeling full from the night before. So down I go, getting greeted by all the friendly staff. I sit down at the only table that's set and it is set for one. I am poured mango juice (spot on) and given papaya fruit (that I didn't enjoy so much, I isn't really to my liking but I managed to eat it all) then I was asked how I wanted my eggs – I went with scrambled. It comes out with bread, butter and jam. I ate all the scrambled egg but it was all a bit too much for me.

Then up to the room where I sat on the porch for a bit and looked at the amazing view before me. When I saw the car making its way up I grabbed my bags and walked to the main building arriving at the same time as the car. One of the women came running up to me because I was carrying my bags, bless her. I told her I was fine but she wasn't having any of it. She helped me to the car where it was loaded in. Her name is Happy and her name suits her perfectly as she has a great big smile.

Then we headed for Ruwaha National Park. We went to the campsite first, where I was shown to my room. It is like a little tin hut (called a Banda). There are several bandas set out not too far from each other. I was lucky to have the only banda that had its own bathroom attached to it. You will see why that is REALLY amazing as I am told while being shown to my banda that I cannot leave it once it is dark without a park ranger, as there is so much wildlife wandering through the camp at night (elephant, cheetah, lions etc). The toilets are by the main building so for everyone else it is a call to the park ranger to come to their banda to accompany them to the toilets. The park rangers carry guns and tranquilizers for protection.

I dump my bags in my room and meet Salim back at the car. Cook stays at the camp to start prep work for dinner as Salim and I head of to start the game drive.

It was absolutely amazing. I really cannot give it justice in words. First we see impala – beautiful creatures. I love how graceful they are and when they run and leap, it is so amazing to watch.

Very quickly after that we see a giraffe and then we saw a few more straight after. They are such remarkable animals. And when you watch them you can see they are actually a bit dumb. It is like you can see their thought process – should I stay here or should I run, then you can almost see them coming to their conclusion. It is really funny to experience.

We also came across two giraffes fighting over a female. It is such a sight to see them doing that. They use the horns on their head and go for each other's necks. It crazy to see how they swing their head round to get to the other giraffes' neck.

We then came across elephants and at one point we were so unbelievably close to a whole herd of elephants and they were covering themselves in mud (they do this for a couple of reasons, one it cools them down, second it protects their skin and thirdly when the mud dries and they scratch themselves on the bark of trees the mud comes off taking ticks that got stuck in the mud with them) and seeing the baby elephants (calves) covering themselves in mud was too cute to watch.

Then at one point we were driving past a smaller herd of elephants (with some calves) and they were right by the track so we were getting so close but one of the mums didn't like it and started blowing her trunk (they are exceptionally loud) and she was pushing her baby behind her and getting to closer to us. I did start to panic at one point that she was going to charge us but she moved back a bit and we drove on. It was so amazing though.

Through some of that parts we drove through there was hundreds of baboon in a big pack and at one point we witnessed two of them fighting, which was a spectacular thing to see.

We were incredibly close to some zebra. They are elegant animals and almost hypnotizing to watch.

Throughout the day we saw so many giraffe and right near the end we got so close to one I could have touched it.

To my joy we also found lions. It is amazing to come across one pride never mind more. Altogether we had four sightings of lion which is phenomenal. The first pride we came across we could have driven right past without seeing them if it hadn't been for the half eaten giraffe carcass. That set off a light to keep our eyes open as they would be close by guarding the rest of their meal. Sure enough there they were hidden right by it in the bushes, relaxing in the shade after their big feed and wow were they a sight to see. I was mesmerized. The adult male wasn't to be seen but a young male and young female were there with several adult females. We could also make out two little cubs. It really was so marvelous.

Then later on we found a male from another pride. What power he demanded. He was so breathtaking to watch. The sheer size of him! I just stood there, poking out the top of the safari jeep looking down over the bridge staring at this wonderful animal below me. So very close and so gorgeous. I took several photos before I look just up the valley and there by a big tree lying in the shade were the lionesses and cubs. I couldn't believe I was seeing two prides in one day. It really was so fantastic to see. We stayed there for a while watching the cubs moving around and playing a bit with one another, when we saw the lionesses and cubs start to move we drove round and followed alongside them for a while – it would seem they were ready for food and it was time to go on a hunt. I wished we could have followed them all day and watched but you can't drive just anywhere in the park, there are tracks in order to stop wildlife being too interrupted.

When we stopped for our lunch there was a giraffe standing so close to us on our right and in front of us (but a bit further away) were more giraffes. Not a bad view while eating. There was a brave wee squirrel (much smaller and cuter than ours back in the UK) that kept coming up looking for food. At one point he was brave and he sat on my leg. I wish I could have gotten a photo but as soon as I moved even a fraction he ran.

Then all of a sudden just to our right a few elephants walked past, you know just your typical lunch scenery. I mean can you really believe it, an elephant walked right past me as I sat their eating a sandwich.

While we were stopped for our lunch Salim told me how he had been at boarding school here and how the older kids would beat them and steal their sugar (you see they had horrible food and the only thing that made it better was to sprinkle some sugar on top so for them it was a valuable item) and how the teachers would beat them with sticks as punishment.

We also saw jackal, buffalo, hippos and crocodiles. Seeing all these animals in their natural environment was so tremendous to see and they were so mesmerizing to watch. I just love it.

We saw so many beautiful and interesting birds (including an eagle, vultures and crowned hornbills to name a few). Then all the colourful and fascinating bugs, insects and lizards.

Just at the end we heard thunder but it was so loud – like really crazy loud, like I have never heard before loud. We saw some flashes of lightning. It was so incredible to see that on my right there was blue sky with a few fluffy white clouds and then on my left there was dark skies, grey cloud and lightning.

It was all in all such a remarkable day.

Me in the Safari Jeep

So when I got back to the camp I went off to my banda and lay on my bed going through the photos from the day – incredible by the way. The park ranger came to get me to walk me over for dinner. Already there were four people sitting round the table. I felt a bit awkward at first but soon everyone started to chat to each other. They were nice people, 2 from Israel and 2 from Prague. We were served some soup then some meat (again I had no idea what it was and I thought best not to ask) with rice. The people were nice and seemed so shocked I was on a solo trip. I have had that reaction a lot. I guess it is quite a rare thing over here.

Now I am under my mosquito net hoping this one will work properly; using my wee torch to write my days events. My eyes are getting heavy now, it's been a magnificent but tiring day. I am surrounded by the sound of nature; the insect noises and who knows what other animals I may hear during the night. So time to turn off my torch and get some rest.

It is proper pitch black here, just like at Hill Top Lodge last night. I understand now what my parents meant when they told me about their stories from living here.

My favourite story that my mum and dad told me from their time here in Tanzania was about one night when they were getting ready to go to a function on one of the HMS ships that was in port.

These functions were always a dress up occasion, where they would be invited on board for a dinner. This one night they had got ready to go, dressed and dolled up. However for some reason that night my mum's skin felt irritated. She was so uncomfortable that she decided to go wash her face and the make-up off. She washed her face and then dried it off in a towel. But to her horror when she opened her eyes she could not see a thing. She shouted on my dad, screaming for my dad to come quick because she had gone blind. Panicking and her mind racing, she thought about how she would get on and off the plane, how she would never see anyone again) she got angry when she could hear my dad laughing beside her. Angrily she asked what was so funny, he replied between laughs that there had been a black out and she hadn't gone blind. That is how dark it is here. As you can imagine my dad told that story to everyone that night. Poor mum, but it is so funny. She tells me it much better than me though.

Thirty

I had a fabulous last few days before I left for the journey to Tanzania. Brijan and I were going for walks every night along the boardwalk and having a good laugh and talking about the future and what lay ahead. Of course there was lots of talk about my impending trip and I am sure he called me crazy or words along those lines a few times.

Having a few nights out with some of our friends at Olivia's Bar was fun and life was pretty perfect in general. It just seemed to get better day by day and I was so happy.

I got myself packed for my trip checking over and over I had everything that was essential. I was getting super excited now for the trip and it was beginning to feel less like a dream and a little more real though I still couldn't totally believe I was really doing this.

So my last night Brijan cooked me dinner, we went for a walk along the boardwalk having a good laugh and giggle. There are a cluster of 5 stars in the sky that we always look for that looks like a smile. We said that when I am in Africa I can always look at the stars and know that Brijan will be looking at the same ones in Holland (he was heading home for 3 weeks with his family) and it was a comfort to know I will always have that. When we got home we watched a film before going to bed.

The next morning I got up and double checked I had everything, had a quick something to eat and printed my ticket. Brijan and I went for a walk in the sun by the beach and talked about the things we would get up to when we got back. Then it was home, shower, get my suitcase and head for the bus.

Thirty One

11th December 2015 20:03

Wow last night was such an incredible experience. I woke up because I could hear something scratching on the roof, they did say how the animals came into camp a lot and how those that can get to the roof often eat berries that had fallen from the trees off them. So I got out of bed and grabbed my torch and shone it out the window to see if I could see anything. I was completely taken aback when there right in front of me was an elephants leg and body. I wasn't exactly expecting that.

Then to wake up this morning to hear lions roaring. Can you imagine? To open your eyes to a pink and red sky as the sun is just starting to rise and you can hear lions calling to each other. It is the most wonderful experience. I got up and looked out my window to see the most striking sky, I wish I could have got it on camera but the colours just didn't quite come through.

So I get my shower and organized and I head to the main building to have breakfast. Mango and scrambled egg. The land cruiser was packed up and we set off for Udzungwa.

We stopped an hour short of the place for lunch (oh and we bought a corn on the cob off a kid on the street – which I was hesitant to eat with the fear of it not being totally sanitary). Not much of real excitement happened on the drive. We saw some baboon but that

115

was about it. Though we did stop a little place for a toilet break. I went round the back to the toilets and went in. It was an utter dive but you got to do what you got to do. When I tried to get out the toilet the door wouldn't open. I started to panic but I was trying to stay calm and take deep breathes. There were no gaps, full walls and a full door. So with no escape except through the door which totally refused to open. After what seemed like hours (but must have been minutes) I decided to kick the door open and then quickly scurry back to the car.

Then as we were driving through the wee villages to the huts, they pointed out the sugar cane field which is absolutely massive and they pointed out the waterfall I would be going to.

So I was checked into the Hondo Hondo camp. The guy took me up to the mud hut (with a thatched roof) that I am staying in tonight. As he showed me round he told me that the mud keeps it cool (but I can assure you there is nothing cool about it – it is stiflingly hot and I am constantly covered in a thin layer of sweat). The toilet is a little shack just across from my mud hut. It totally reminded me of Shrek's toilet and when the guy then went on to mention there being a resident donkey (which you are not allowed to feed) it did make me chuckle.

He also warned me to be careful when I leave the hut at night as there are wild animals that come through here too but usually baboons and you have to be careful of them during the day too.

Salim then took me to go on my hike. First he drove me down to an office where you sign up and pay to go on the walk and pick up a guide. Then you drive back in the opposite direction for about 10 minutes to the entrance of the walk.

I am not able to tell you my guides name as it was really difficult for me to pronounce never mind write. He is 22 years old and been doing this for 4 months. So we walked 1.6km uphill to the view point and wow is it beautiful. You can see the wonderful

Sanje waterfall (that is actually what Sanje means – wonderful). It was terribly hot and the humidity was through the roof, making the hiking really uncomfortable and making breathing difficult. I was soaked right through. Then we walked down (and a few ups) to go to the plunge pool at the bottom of the waterfall. It is marvelous. So I went for a little swim (though I was nervous about snakes despite being assured there were none). It was a bit awkward though, just the two of us, in a lovely setting and I am stripped down to a swimsuit swimming in a plunge pool while he sits with his feet in watching me. So I didn't stay as long as I would have liked and I didn't get the photos I would have wanted as it seemed a bit uncomfortable.

Then it was a little hike up the hill back to the view point before downhill back to the entrance. Downhill was no problem though it was still unbearably hot and sticky. The hike up had admittedly been really tough.

So it was back to Hondo Hondo camp. I was feeling a bit sick, I just too much heat exposure and food. They make me way more than I would normally eat. So I informed them I wouldn't be eating that night and I just had my Forever shake back in the room.

When I had got back to my hut, I stripped off trying to cool my body down. I was so damn hot and the humidity didn't seem to be giving up. So I grabbed my towel and toiletries and walked down to the shower hut near the entrance. If you don't go while the sun has been on the water tank it will be just really cold water (the man told me about this when he showed me to the hut). Plus I felt horrible and hoped the shower would help. So I showered and back to my mud hut. I stripped off again as soon as I got in, sweating again already. I grabbed my notepad and pen and chilled out on my bed and this is where I plan to spend the rest of the evening. Chilling, listening to the birds, monkeys, insects and noises of the jungle. I can hear thunder in the distance and see some lightning light up the sky so there could be some rain headed this way.

Sanje Waterfalls

My Mud Hut

Thirty Two

On getting back to Edinburgh from Tanzania I had a two days with my mum who had now flown in from Dubai and my brother, sister-in-law and niece. It was nice to have some time with them and to wash my clothes properly in the machine.

On my last day I was told we had to go pick up my sister-in-law's mum from the airport. I wasn't exactly happy that on the day I was to fly out I had to go to the airport to pick her up as it isn't much to get a taxi. We were standing waiting for her to come out the gate and I said I would pop to the toilet and my mum said not to go because she might not recognize Joanne. I thought this was weird especially as I have only seen Joanne a few times and my mum has met her and known her for years. But I waited around.

Next thing I know my dad walks out the gate. I was so shocked I was frozen in place but my wee head raced so fast. I was going oh my god turn and tell mum, dad has come to surprise us all, hang on does she know, am I still to look for Joanne, oh my god I can't believe my dad is here. I finally managed to move and gave my dad a massive hug as the tears trickled down my face.

Apparently they were all in on it to surprise me. I am not usually the one people do surprises for and I couldn't believe everyone had done this. I was getting to see my dad just before Christmas and with my birthday being the next day it was the best present I could ask for. I wasn't sure when I was going to see my dad again and it was just the best thing I could ever ask for.

We had 8 hours so we made the most of our time together and I made sure I got lots of pappy hugs.

Thirty Three

12th December 2015 22:36

Another early rise this morning and I after a very disturbed night's sleep I headed down to the shower hut to refresh myself after what was a very hot and humid evening. It was extremely cold and the sun obviously hadn't been hitting down on it for some time, but the coldness was actually really refreshing and helped me to wake up.

So last night I lay in my bed chilling out. I thought I would get a nice early night and good rest but that wasn't the case. We ended up having a thunder and lightning storm on and off nearly the whole night (though it was needed and made this morning's weather a lot more pleasant). The rain was chucking it down with incredible force and the thunder was so loud you couldn't hear anything else. In between the spurts of thunder, lightning and rain you could hear all the animals moving around and calling to each other. It was quite an experience but I would be lying if I didn't admit there were a few times when I was a little scared that the wee hut I was staying in wasn't quite safe enough in the storm but I needn't have worried.

So as I went to bed so early but wasn't actually sleeping at one point during the night I had to go to the toilet. So I waited till there was a gap in the storm and carefully got out my mosquito net as with the rain insects are more drawn in to the dry places and before I got into bed I had seen enough insects around anyway (including 2 wee geckoes I named Dot and Spot due to their markings), then with my little torch I got my towel on (as I had stripped off due to the heat and humidity) and my slipped my feet into my trainers. I got to the door and took a couple deep breathes before poking my torch out first, having a good look to make sure there were no animals around, though it is so hard to do when it is pitch black and your surrounded by a jungle!

When I had had as good a look as possible I quickly ran over to the toilet hut (I may have made some screechy noises in my frenzy) but also before going in there you have to pop your torch and head in to make sure there are no animals lurking (especially with the rain, they could be taking shelter). But with the all clear I quickly went to the loo and followed the same procedure to get back safely to my wee hut (which was now my sanctuary and actually not being able to see everything just where the wee beam off light from my torch landed was probably a blessing because I don't think I wanted to know what all I was actually sharing my hut with. Geckoes don't bother me, but certain insects, spiders and heaven forbid a snake would make me feel a bit uncomfortable).

I am sure you get the gist of my tiredness this morning. But after my refreshing shower and with semi-clean clothes on I headed to an area set up as an eating area, though we are in the jungle so your little walk is interesting when 3 baboons run right in front of you, so close they nearly run into you. Then as I sat having my breakfast (freshly cut fruit with a glass of mango juice) a whole group of baboons went sauntering past with the babies clinging onto their mummy's tummies. It was such a sight to see. Not quite the breakfast I have standing in my kitchen in Spain of a morning.

Then it was time to start our journey back to Dar Es Salaam. It was far less eventful on our journey home. The only excitement was as we drove back through Mikumi and we could see some of the animals along the drive. Though we didn't see as many on as on the way through last time. I did get a closer glance at some buffalo and we saw some vultures feeding again (I think it was buffalo but I am not entirely sure). But I loved seeing what I could.

The rest of the trip was in near silence as nobody did much talking. I think we were all feeling pretty shattered after a restless night. Nobody could be expected to get a good sleep with that storm overhead. We stopped at one point to stretch our legs and eat our packed lunch. It was the one time in the whole journey I let my pickiness win over and I couldn't bear to eat the tuna sandwich (I just detest even the smell of it) so I hid it in my bag so as not to offend, but ate the rest.

I got to my new hotel called White Sands at about 5.45pm. I arrived and thanked and tipped my driver and Chef. So into the hotel, checked in and into my room. It was very nice, clean and modern rooms. You really couldn't complain though for me I preferred the character of Bahari Beach. This hotel room could be anywhere in the world if you know what I mean (don't get me wrong, still lovely). I got my stuff into my room and got changed and went for a little walk to see round the hotel. I had accidently got a car tan on the drive home, so I am a bit red on one arm and one side of my face (silly girl).

Then back in my room a little while later where I washed all my clothes and hung them up to dry around the room and outside. I have just made myself a Forever shake and I am snuggled in bed. Time for a good sleep now.

Thirty Four

As the plane touched into Malaga I was happy to be home. It was incredible being away and what a remarkable experience I had but it is also nice to get back to your home, friends and life.

Once in my flat I gave it a good clean, got the food shopping in and all my things got put away. Brijan would be home in a few days and just after that his little sister, his mum and her boyfriend would arrive for Christmas.

I went about getting the presents I had bought in the UK wrapped and under the tree. Although I was excited to buy things for everyone I was still feeling the guilt of how privileged I am, so was so glad I had done all the shopping before my trip.

The next day it was my Birthday. I didn't do much that day. I met my sis for a twix milkshake at our usual spot 'El Deseo' in La Cala and had a chat and we decided what we would wear that evening as our staff Christmas night out with Legends Bar fell on my birthday. It was a great night where we got dressed up, went to an amazing show called the 'Chamber of Secrets' in Torremolinos (a mixture of magic, comedy and some singing) then Chinese for dinner before drinking and dancing at Maxxy's. Well we went to a bar called POGS first but it wasn't what we were looking for so we decided to try Maxxys. However most of the girls had dropped off by then and it was just Charlotte, myself, Paul and

Andrea (Bar Dad and Bar Mum – the owners of Legends). Oh what a laugh and giggle we had in Maxxy'.s Danced the night away and we were the last four to get chucked out at the end hehe.

It was a fabulous night followed by a few days of hairdressing as everyone got themselves ready for Christmas. Then Brijan came home. It was so great to see him after 3 weeks. I have never gone that long without seeing him since the day we met (and I hope I never have to again). As you can imagine there was a lot of chat about Tanzania but also a lot of chat about the next couple weeks as there was a lot to look forward to.

The next day I was helping to clean up Legends after part of the refurb had been done and then off to a client to do her hair, then quickly home for another client and clean up as fast as possible as Brijan's family were due to arrive in the evening after driving down from Holland with our new puppies.

As I walked in to the flat on returning from my client, I was in a rush as I was a little late in getting back and my client was due to arrive at mine any minute. Brijan met me at the door and then my ears pricked as I thought I heard a dog. I looked at him and I saw his smile and I knew they were here already. I asked anyway though before running to the balcony where I saw my little puppies Rocky and Bentley running round and barking (at me) with little present bows on their collars. Too cute. I was so happy and excited, it killed me that my client arrived right then and I had to carry on with work.

The next week was great. I love my puppies and we had such a great time with the family. I love his mum and sister so much and we had such a laugh together. I can't believe his ten year old sister can wear my shoes (much to her pleasure when she saw all my high heels) and is almost the height of me!

Once Brijan's family left it was time for us to settle into our new routine with our wee puppies.

Thirty Five

13th December 2015 21.28

My final day in Tanzania has been a very chilled and nice day. I was up at 5.45am after my early night and knowing that it was too early to go for breakfast I started to sort my case out as I fly tomorrow. I got my now handwashed and air dried clothes and separated them into my case and a bag for leaving for the housecleaning team as they were not necessary for me to take home. With only the bits left out that I will need to use between now and when I go I was looking pretty organized for flying home.

I went down for my breakfast, a buffet where I had some bacon, fresh fruit and a croissant. I then headed to the swimming pool where I chilled for the rest of the day. I only left there for lunch which I had with Lisa and Steve, who drove to the hotel to meet me. I am glad to say Lisa was looking much better though she was not 100%. She never did tell me what it was she got.

They asked lots of questions about my safari and we discussed my plans for proceeding to help out with Beta. They are sewn into my heart now and I will do all I can for as long as I can to help them. I really do hope that at some point we will be able to make them self sufficient and not depend on others. After a long but lovely lunch we said our goodbyes and I know we will keep in touch.

At the end of my day I went back to my room and got showered and headed to the bar. I wasn't feeling so hungry after a big lunch so I just ordered a snack and a coca cola. As I sat it suddenly started chucking it down with rain, so I ordered another coke to ride it out a bit before heading back to my room. My plan was to put a film on and relax but the power has been cutting on and off so I think I will just try and get some sleep. It has been an emotional ride since getting here and to be honest my head hasn't stopped racing. I have so much I want to do and achieve, part of me really cant wait to get home and start putting things into place. The next step to help Beta needs to happen already!

Thirty Six

This whole experience has shown me how lucky we are to have everything we do. We take so much for granted in our lives. It is the day to day things we would feel the most if they were taken away; like running water, clean water, food. Yet it astonishes me just how much we complain. We have it so easy. Don't get me wrong, no matter who you are or what your circumstances are we all go through hard times and we all learn to deal with things different. I do believe however that we need to start counting our blessings and teach the generations to follow how to be grateful for what they have.

As I sat in Abu Dhabi airport waiting for my flight back to Edinburgh, I heard one little girl who could be no older that 7, sat there decked in a lovely little outfit, with ugg boots playing on an I-pad that she needed a Galaxy Tablet because her brother has one. Her mum said to her but you have an I-pad, the childs response was AND? I don't have one of them so I need one too.

I sat there thinking to myself, she has no idea how good she has it. She has been treated to a holiday abroad, no doubt taken out to fun places, no doubt got spoilt, she has nice clothes to wear, a rucksack full if sweets and chocolate (I witnessed this) and is playing on an I-pad. I have just left kids that go days without food, no clean clothes and hardly any that aren't torn but still make the most of what they have got.

It is about time we changed our attitude. Maybe our world would be a happier place if we learnt a little more gratitude. I always strive to do better but I am happy with what I have. I am thankful for the life I lead and for everything I have.

I don't pretend to be perfect. I have my down days, the days where I complain, the days I feel sorry for myself but I don't have many of them and when I do I try and remind myself of how lucky I am to have the opportunity in life that I have been given.

Thirty Seven

14ᵗʰ December 2015 23.00

I am currently sitting in the airport in Abu Dhabi and can't quite believe how much has happened since I sat here a couple of weeks ago. Got 6 hours to wait between my flights, but it isn't too bad. I have had a wonder round and grabbed something to eat. I plan to read my diary back after I write this passage as I wait for my flight.

I was up early getting showered and the last of my packing done. Even lighter travelling back now I have left a lot here and used up my Forever powder and toiletries and I thought I had travelled light coming here. I was actually so lightly travelled that the guy at check in said there was no point me checking my trolley bag in as it was so light, just to take it on board.

Anyway, I had my breakfast got my bags and headed to reception to get the taxi I had preordered only to find out they had forgot to do it and said they could get me a last minute one but they cost more. Now I am no idiot and I told the woman quite frankly that it was their mistake if this was the case, so she would arrange a taxi for me and I would pay the same price end of story. This is exactly what happened. I have to say though, in my whole trip this is the only time someone tried to underhand me which surprised me, as there are so many warnings about this kind of thing happening in the country (and I don't doubt that it does).

I set off nice and early as the traffic can be so awful and it says it can take up to 2 hours in the traffic to get to the airport from the hotel. But of course I go there in 25 minutes so now had 4 hours of waiting to do. Dar Es Salaam airport is tiny, so there was really nothing to do but sit and wait. The desk hadn't opened yet for my flight due to my extreme earliness.

As I sat and waited the power cut out several times. I have become accustomed to this in Tanzania though it is a tad unsettling at an airport. When finally I got to check in, as I said before I was told to just keep my bag and I was sent towards passport control. I had to fill in a little form to exit the country and then up the stairs to departures where your luggage is screened before getting to the "lounge" area.

I bought a little book for my niece, which I think was lovely. The most expensive thing I bought on my whole trip! I hope she will love it though. Maybe it will put the intrigue of travel and Africa into her as it was put in me hearing all the stories of parents' life here.

I got a little doze on my flight into Abu Dhabi and watched some Love Actually, getting myself back into Christmas spirit, though I feel so far parted from that feeling right now. I am sure it won't take me long to get it, I have always had a big Christmas spirit.

Thirty Eight

I have had so much positive feedback from the Ball and so many people have said they can't wait till November, that I have decided that I can't wait till then either. I am desperate to raise more money and get on with what needs to be done in Beta that there is no way I can sit on my bum and wait till the end of the year. Besides I think it makes sense to get something going off the back of my trip, to let people know I have just been there, what it is like and why we so desperately need to help.

I also don't want it all to be exactly the same, so I have decided to arrange a Garden Party instead. Still a food and live entertainment based event but an outdoor one with a more casual atmosphere. November can be the ball setting. I live in Spain, I am as well making the most of the good weather here.

So here I go again, setting about making arrangements for another event and I only have 3 months to organize it all, but it is all worth it. Hopefully it won't be long before I get to go back to Beta.

Printed in the United States
By Bookmasters